Winners Win and Losers Lose

Everyone wants to be a winner. But only a few succeed. This inspirational new guide helps readers understand what separates the men from the boys, the sheep from the goats and the winners from the losers. The authors explain how to prepare and plan for success, both in business and personal lives and avoid all those pitfalls lurking along the way threatening to turn would-be winners into dreaded losers.

Nick Thornely and **Dan Lees**, the co-authors have collaborated on a number of best-selling guides aimed at helping people achieve their true potential.

Suhel Seth, the **Foreword** writer, is the CEO of Equus Red Cell, a leading Advertising and Communications company. That apart Mr. Seth is a well-known columnist and panelist, as well as a theatre and television celebrity.

Other Roli Business Book Titles

Confessions of Shameless Self Promoters *Foreword:* DILIP CHERIAN	DEBBIE ALLEN
52 Ways To Motivate Your Staff *Foreword:* PRADIP CHANDA	TRISH NICHOLSON
Getting It Right The Second Time *Foreword:* SHUNU SEN	MICHAEL GERSHMAN
Making A Difference *Foreword:* S. BUDHIRAJA & A. MALHOTRA	BRUCE DIXON
The Money Launderers *Foreword:* KALYAN RUDRA	BOB BLUNDEN

Winners Win and Losers Lose

Nick Thornely and Dan Lees

Foreword by
Suhel Seth

Business
Roli Books

Business Collection

Cartoons featured in this book by Adrian Dixon

Published in 2001 by
Management Books 2000 Ltd, U.K.
First Published in India by Roli Books Pvt. Ltd., 2003
under license from Management Books 2000 Pvt. Ltd., U.K.
Roli Books Pvt. Ltd.
M-75, G.K. II (Market)
New Delhi 110 048
Phones: 26442271, 26462782, 26460886
Fax: 26467185
E-mail: roli@vsnl.com; Website: rolibooks.com
Also at
Varanasi, Agra, Jaipur and the Netherlands

ISBN: 81-7436-256-8
Rs. 195

Typeset in Minion by Roli Books Pvt. Ltd. and
printed at Paul Press, Okhla, New Delhi-110 020

Contents

Editor's Note

It is infuriating but true. Success seems to chase successful people while failures appear to pile up on the hapless ones. And of course, we admire and respect winners and are embarrassed in the presence of losers.

It's not that the world wants to be unkind to losers, that just happens. And as a result all of us want to be winners. Rightly so. The next logical step is to prepare to be a winner. That's where this somewhat unusual book helps the reader identify what makes a winner and chalk out a path to making winning a habit.

We asked Suhel Seth to write a Foreword not just because he epitomises a winner in whatever he does, but because of the insights he has gained into the minds of some of the winners he has personally interacted with. As he says 'You don't have to be a genius to emerge a winner: you need to have the challenger mindset: where you challenge every known premise' including the one that holds that winners are born, not made.

Just change your mindset to change your life for the better. As the authors of the book point out, even winning at tiddlywinks will help you get into the winning habit, and that will help you become a winner elsewhere, at office for example. Go ahead, try it, you have nothing to lose but the habit of losing.

Pradip Chanda

Acknowledgements

This book is dedicated to Dan and Molly Lees, who played a crucial part in writing the first 'Winner' series. Dan was one of those people who was always cheerful and never missed a deadline. His idea of pleasure was to write and write, and he always wrote his 1,000 words a day and more.

I heard about Dan through his *Champagne Fitness* book and we agreed to work together on *How to Be a Winner*. I liked his winning idea that, if you had to diet to lose weight, then it was preferable to enjoy eating a small number of luxury items like smoked salmon, rather than consistently cutting down on food quantities at regular meals. I also liked his concept of drinking champagne instead of beer as an attempt to maintain the social pleasures of life, and lose weight at the same time.

Dan and I spent many happy hours at his house in Bristol and later in France.

I know that he would approve of *Winners Win and Losers Lose.*

Dan was a real winner and 'happy in his skin'.

Foreword

The Victorious Inherit the Earth

In days of yore, this would've sounded almost heretical, but the truth of the matter is that we all respect winners. We respect them for what they've achieved; we convert their winning formulae into management books, and hope that their knowledge will sit easily on our shoulders so that we can follow in their footsteps.

Winning is something each one of us desires, but we'd rather be spoon-fed than fight for, condition ourselves to, then go on to accomplish what we want. That is why, time and again, I have underscored the fact that you don't need to be a genius to emerge a winner. What is necessary, though, is a mindset where you challenge every known premise, cross every barrier that is erected in your way, and vow to scale the summit of the very last blue mountain.

Winners are in essence challengers: they suffer from divine discontent, and hate status quo. Like Robert Frost, they are always attempting to walk the least trodden path. That, I guess, explains why we have only so few winners. In fact, every race has place for only one winner—the rest are losers. And they are losers not because the world wishes to be unkind to them, but, simply because they have just not won.

Winning in life is an art. And embedded in that art is a deep understanding of what you want to achieve in precise terms. Winners are always focused. They are almost always certain of their goals, and rarely change tack. The problem with people either in the corporate world today, or in their personal lives, is a singular lack of focus—we wish to be all things to all people. The riches lie, however, in niches, and not in being a generalist hoping to grab as much of the pie as one possibly can.

Winners treat every move in life as one would in a game of chess. Therefore the beginning has to be as adroit as the conclusion. That is the fundamental approach of winners. Winners do not set targets on a daily basis, but almost on a minute-to-minute basis. And their targets are not set on paper. These are, in fact, inscribed in their whole being. Take a look at those who've won in life. They have won because they have been remarkably focused, and have had a deep sense of conviction, which brings me to the next trait of winners.

Winners in the world are devoutly paranoid. They are constantly seeking to accomplish something new, not because they crave recognition, but because they are driven by their deepest convictions. Winners are obsessive about success, and don't just sit around waiting for it to happen. This is something that they realise very early in life. For them, life is not a journey to be completed at leisure—they set exacting milestones for themselves, and strict deadlines to conquer all they must. Thus, focus and conviction become an integral part of their being. These are not mere appendages to their persona, but a part of their DNA. Unfortunately, only a few people are capable of appreciating that.

Let us take a look at some classic Indian winners, be it in the field of politics or, closer to the subject of this book, in business.

India attained freedom because of the doggedness of one man who wasn't scared to take on the might of the British Empire simply because it came in the way of his winning. For Mohandas Karamchand Gandhi, victory was a long-standing ambition, which he wanted to savour without any hindrance. While he was certainly a villain for the honchos of the Raj, there is enough documented evidence to suggest that he did have his share of admirers amidst the colonialists as well. This, in effect, is the hallmark of true winners. They always manage to command the admiration and respect of their adversaries. Albeit silent, the admiration and respect are certainly substantial.

Through their deeds, winners leave behind legacies, which far outlive their lifetimes. It suffices to examine India's corporate horizon, to clearly see that many heroes were born without much fanfare, yet they managed to carve out and hold a place of their own.

When Karsanbhai Mehta started selling loose detergent powder on handcarts, those at Hindustan Levers who dismissed him as `that trader of inferior yellow powder' were legion. But when the history of fast-moving consumer goods in India is written, Karsanbhai's name shall mark a watershed. And not so much for making Nirma the household brand that it is today, but more for the relentlessness with which he laced his pursuit. It is that dint and diligence, which will illuminate those pages of documented history. Karsanbhai's success story corroborates the fact that getting fazed is anathema to a winner.

Winners in India are like winners elsewhere in the world. For them, geographies are on paper, their borders ever-expanding. One such visionary in the Indian context was Aditya Vikram Birla from the Birla clan. He set up plants and factories in distant lands only because he was undaunted by global competition. So whether it was with polyester or palm oil, Aditya showed to every Indian, the path to global nirvana on the one hand, global respect on the other.

In fact, the secret of winning in life lies in seeing life differently—in its various hues, with its various ramifications. Life becomes a path that leads to achievements. Winners do not value life as much as what they can do with it. For them life is not a tedious journey from the womb to the tomb. It is a journey about crossing milestones and looking forward to new ones. I have often believed that winners erect barriers themselves to experience the thrill of breaking them down, and even in the face of adversity, do not hesitate to build empires from dust, like some of those who came to India after Partition did.

The founder of Escorts, H.P. Nanda is a case in point. He came, he saw, he built. Escorts was the vision of a winner, not a business blueprint that emerged from the mind of a consultant. When everyone around H.P. Nanda was turning a blind eye to opportunities, it was precisely his ability to carve out a vision that made Escorts the household name that it finally became. And he embarked on the journey when he was already quite old. This then brings me to yet another trait of winners.

Winners neither seek refuge in their lack of experience, nor in the burden of their years. They strike whenever they believe they are ready. A look at Dhirubhai Ambani's trajectory proves that we have an ageless wonder before us—a man who invented desire for every Indian, the desire to reap a golden harvest from one's investments. And Dhirubhai came back to India from Aden, disproving the general belief that success lies beyond the shores of India. He showed the world that India was an exciting land, living in an exciting age, with endless opportunities for those with grit and determination. It is this combination of grit and determination that has made Reliance what it is today.

There have been other winners as well, winners who have won with aplomb in their chosen fields, be it Swami Agnivesh, Mother Teresa, Amartya Sen or V.S. Naipaul. They have had more than just courage of conviction. They have had the courage to achieve, a courage born of the courage to fulfill whatever they had set out to achieve. They have been marathon runners. For them the 100-metre sprint was only an indicator of capability: the true measure of success lay far beyond.

Through time, and geographical expanses, we have seen the winner both as a hero and a villain. Gandhi too evoked a mixed response. Here, I must point out yet another common denominator in winners—the means almost never matter for them. All that matters is the end, and the fact that they achieve the end, the pressure, hurdles, or social constraints notwithstanding, which is why people like Raja Rammohun Roy or the late M.S. Oberoi are such terrific heroes. They dared to dream. Achievement, not failure stared them in the face. And this is yet something else that winners share: across the world, winners have been dreamers, consumed every passing minute by the burning desire to realize their dreams. Paranoid about losing grasp over their dreams, they tend to be self-deprecatory, but only to a point. Their essential hallmark is their ability to dream, and inspire people to dare to dream their dreams, which is why almost all winners make great leaders, although the same may not be true the other way round.

Humanity has never been short on inspiration. We have been inspired by thinkers, scientists and politicians alike: we have been captivated by their vision of the world, and that vision is so charming that we have almost never questioned these visionaries. You inspire others when you can make them feel the way you do, when the strength of your conviction overrides considerations like reason and convention. If convention made this world go round, then the Industrial Revolution would never have happened, and Einstein would have remained a footnote in history. Gorbachev did not free the world from the cold war; he showed his own people a world they never imagined they could ever be part of. He was a winner in a true sense. He challenged established conventions much in the same way as Nelson Mandela did or, for that matter, Steve Jobs continues to do.

Bill Gates has been widely criticized due to the anti-trust litigation. Much as people in his industry would despise him, there is never any doubt in anyone's mind that Bill Gates is, and will remain, a winner, and that a single errant e-mail will not change any of this. It is this realisation with which we must come to terms.

Losing is as much about a lack of focus and principles as is winning. Losers are neither meant to earn our sympathy, nor even perhaps our scorn. Yet winners inspire faith and belief, losers elicit sympathy and scorn. So what would you much rather be? Someone who believes life is a spectator sport, and is, therefore, content with participating in it, or a person who is of the opinion that life is a race to be won?

Winning is eventually about courting the unthinkable, doing perhaps the unmentionable and scaling the insurmountable, because winners never worry about defeat. They uproot the fear of defeat from their beings forever. After that, life is about accomplishing what one has set out to accomplish, not about offering excuses or apologies for one's failings!

In today's exceedingly competitive world, you need to change your mindset before you can change your life for the better. You need to be selfish, and yes, almost all winners are. They are selfish because they are not looking for community healing. There's an excellent saying by David Ogilvy: 'There are no statues of committees in any parks, only those of individuals,' which is why winners invest their life with a certain degree of selfishness and are unhesitating about doing so. Winners are never accountable to anyone but themselves, which is why there is a certain arrogance about them. Winners dream and dare—both private pastimes, which do not seek peer approval.

So go ahead and win your way through life, and remember winners make this journey alone, without a care in the world. They are only driven by the thought of winning. Nothing else matters. And ideally, nothing else should!

1

Anyone Can Be a Winner

Most of us want to be winners – which isn't too surprising as winners tend to be happier, sexier and more exciting than other people and, while they may or may not be richer, their lives have a champagne sparkle losers can never experience.

While there are innumerable ways in which to become a winner, the best short definition of a winner we can come up with is someone who is 'happy in his or her skin'. These sorts of people can be dukes or dustmen, debs or dressmakers and we can usually spot them at a glance because they have presence, they command respect and they usually appear to be enjoying life a great deal more than most of the folk around them.

Take a look, for example, at the joy on the face of the racing motorist who has roared past the chequered flag to become a champion. As he sprays the applauding spectators with bubbly, he may take a swig from the magnum – but he doesn't need it. He's already drunk with triumph and the realisation that his win will not only bring him increased fame and money but will enable him to take his pick of the best that life has to offer. You can see the same joy on the faces of other obvious winners, like the tycoon who has completed a multi-million pound deal or the actress who has won a coveted role, as they too celebrate their achievements in champagne to accentuate the bubbly, ebullient feeling that winning brings in its train, along with the tireless energy that enables winners to dance the night away while losers slink off home to lick their wounds.

No wonder most of us want to be winners and to put the sparkle into our lives that winning brings. The good news is that, while we may not all make the grade as racing drivers, film stars or tycoons, there is nothing to stop us becoming winners.

Winners like themselves

It's worthwhile reminding ourselves every now and again that we are unique and special because it helps build up our self-esteem. Winners are always keenly aware of their own value. Winners like themselves – it's another way of being 'happy in one's skin' and one of the most valuable attributes of a winner.

It is this self-worth which enables winners to develop a personal comfort zone – a skin thick enough to provide an armour against the world's slings and arrows, often enabling them to ignore the minor worries which seem so important to non-winners and to get on with the business of winning. We will pick up the idea of comfort zones later.

A win is a win is a win

The trouble is that most of us have been conditioned to regard life as a race or contest in which there can be only a few winners, along with one or two runners up, while the rest of us remain sad and unlucky losers. In many ways, this conditioning is the fault of the media whose constant focussing on the glamorous BIG winners persuades many of us that we will never be able to compete, let alone win, and that our lot in life is to sit enviously on the side lines. This, of course, is nonsense and, if winning were confined to the small group whose triumphs receive national or international acclaim, life for most of us would be intolerable.

The fact is that anyone can be a winner – the scale doesn't matter all that much, and the schoolboy who finds a pound coin in his path probably feels more triumph than the multi-millionaire who wins a thousand pounds at the gambling tables.

If we are going to be winners, we have to fight hard against this media inspired conviction that winners are rarities or that there can be 'only one winner'.

Watch the players in the next football match you see and you'll have no difficulty in identifying at least eleven winners when the victorious team does its lap of honour, not to mention the winning manager, the winning trainer and the rest, together with their thousands of 'victorious' fans. Nor does the match have to be a championship game; you only have to think back to your school days to remember the joy of being a member of the school team – or merely belonging to the winning school.

People were experiencing triumph long before there was television or newspapers and long before winning became the apparent prerogative of the rich and famous. Primitive tribesmen, for example, who returned home from the hunt with enough meat to feed their families, were winners in a very real sense and their achievements were duly celebrated by the whole tribe. Today we call people who come home with the wherewithal to feed their families 'breadwinners' and while, for some reason, a disparaging element has crept into the phrase – perhaps because breadwinners are not regarded as being particularly glamorous – they are *winners* and it's perhaps time both they and their families recognised the fact.

Prizes for all

Life is not a race, even though the analogy is a seductive one and may occasionally be useful. In fact, life isn't a sporting contest of any sort, which is just as well since a life with only one winner and only one prize would leave nothing much to live for for the rest of us. Fortunately, in every life – and especially in every working life – there are thousands of prizes to be won, which means that everyone can be a winner and that there are prizes for all of us whether we are bosses or office boys, factory floor workers, secretaries, sales staff or foremen.

The great thing is that to be a winner in the game of life – as opposed to artificial contests, sporting or otherwise – you rarely have to beat any other person in the sense of making them look and feel like losers. In fact, in order to begin winning, the only person you have to beat is *yourself*. For life's real winners, winning works out much more like a bargain than a battle, with all parties feeling they have gained. In other words, everyone finishes up a winner.

The fact is that real winning is holistic and, in the sense that holistic medicine aims to treat the whole body, holistic winning involves winning in every aspect of life, which means that a genuine winner should not only have a healthy mind in a healthy body but a healthy, happy and contented mind in a healthy, happy and contented body.

Holistic winning, then, means winning right across the board rather than confining our wins to one or two specific victories to the exclusion of everything else. The whole person should win and almost always does so in such a way that other people win too.

Holistic winning involves another interesting concept in that it carries with it the idea that the whole is greater than the sum of its parts and in this particular case many small wins add up to something much more important than one would expect the accumulation to achieve. Holistic winners of this sort are often seen as 'Fortune's favourites' or as men and women who 'have everything', the implication being that their being such obvious winners in all respects is a matter of luck, whereas in reality it is usually due to their being able to make the most of whatever possessions and talents they have.

Nothing succeeds like success

There is a lot of truth in the cliché that 'nothing succeeds like success' because being a winner is very much an attitude of mind and one which can be cultivated. As we'll see, winning is a habit and to win even one of life's minor prizes puts you in the running for more and bigger victories.

Getting the winning habit can put a champagne sparkle into our lives that will last for ever, rather than fading away as it may do after a once in a lifetime victory, but acquiring the winning habit may involve a rethink when it comes to identifying our goals.

Winners are always being told how lucky they are, even though they are probably no more fortunate or unfortunate than anyone else. The thing is that winners do, by and large, have an optimistic view of the world, which means that they expect to be lucky, ensuring that when a stroke of good fortune comes along they recognise it and make full use of it.

Identifying goals

Identifying long term goals is a useful exercise and even a little day-dreaming about them can be fun. However, to be obsessed with major goals to the exclusion of everything else can be a recipe for unhappiness, because if you don't achieve your ambition when you feel you should, you are going to be miserable. You'll also worry and, when it comes to winning, worry is counter-productive.

It's much more satisfying – once you've identified your main goal and spent a little time dreaming about how great it would feel to achieve it – to set yourself a number, in fact the largest possible number, of interim targets, the achievement of each one of which counts as a win.

Don't forget, if you do it this way you will have enjoyed any number of victories in the course of pursuing your final goal and, while this will make you much more likely to win through than would otherwise be the case, should you by any chance not win your final goal – say, through circumstances beyond your control – you won't feel anything like as miserable.

A new formula for success

Most people would agree that, on the whole, **Winners are happy – Losers are miserable** which means – if you accept the conventional idea of a winner as the lone, laurel-wreathed victor – a great many of us are condemned to spend our lives in misery, especially at work.

After all, there are always going to be more workers than managing directors and more clerks than office managers. However, if we turn the formula round and say **Happy people are winners – Miserable people are losers** we get a whole new perspective on winning because in any given work situation, there can be any number of happy people and therefore any number of winners – it's up to us to make sure we are among them.

Why do we want to win?

In case anyone thinks that all we have been doing so far is playing around with words, we can now ask ourselves why we want to win and what there is about winning which is going to make us happier? In other words, what are the incentives, provided by ourselves or by others, which will persuade us to aim for a specific goal, the achieving of which we will consider as 'winning'.

Money isn't everything

People who say 'Money isn't everything' usually have enough of the stuff – and are generally talking to people who haven't – so it's not surprising that the phrase is regarded with suspicion, not to say cynicism. However, there is no reason why the idea that there are other sources of satisfaction than money, especially at work, should be rejected out of hand.

Money, of course, can be useful to gratify many of our desires and to provide many different sorts of satisfaction so there's no denying that in the workplace it is a major incentive, if not *the* incentive. It's also a useful measure – although certainly not the only measure – of attainment. This being the case, employers who offer non-financial incentives instead of money can hardly be surprised if their proposals are greeted with suspicion. On the other hand, those who offer non-financial incentives in addition to a fair rate for the job stand a very good chance of employing potential winners and thus becoming winners themselves.

We'll be returning to the subject of money later – in almost any work context, it would be unrealistic not to do so – but for the moment let's accept, if we can, that there are other forms of incentive, other ways in which we ourselves, as well as other people, can persuade us to become winners.

If not money, what?

One of the easiest ways to discover if there are non-financial incentives which would persuade us to strive for any particular goal and to make ourselves winners, is to imagine that we already have all the money in the world, or at least more than enough for our needs. Okay, we might loaf around for a while, maybe even for months, but eventually most of us would begin to crave some form of activity and even if we were to tackle something which, on the face of it, wasn't work – like taking up golf or tennis – we would find ourselves trying to improve our game – trying, in other words, to become winners. In fact, people who become multi-millionaires often do go on working, and working very hard, even though it is difficult to believe that they need more millions or yet another private jet.

… Practical winning

So, you have a million or two – what would be your incentives? Our list is opposite and we'll be looking at some of them in detail later. Perhaps you can add a few of your own. Do not be surprised if your list is a short one, as it may mean you are reasonably content with your lifestyle. Getting more from what you already have is a certain way to feel more like a winner.

WHEN YOU HAVE YOUR MILLIONS, WHAT WOULD YOU DO?

List	*Ideas*
PERSONAL SATISFACTION	Learning to paint watercolour landscapes
A SENSE OF ACHIEVEMENT	Reducing your golf handicap to single figures
CHALLENGE	Climbing the Andes
SOCIAL ADVANCEMENT	Attending a Garden Party at Buckingham Palace
POWER	Going into politics
COMMUNITY SPIRIT	Raising money for charity, e.g. National Trust
STATUS	Owning the biggest swimming pool in your area
SOCIAL CONSCIENCE	Donating money to those less fortunate than yourself
PATRIOTISM	Organising a challenge for the America's Cup
BUILDING SOMETHING FOR THE FUTURE	Funding a museum
PRESTIGE	Becoming chairman of something

Even from this short list, it is obvious that there are many forms of incentive besides the financial and also that many of them are interlinked; several factors, for instance, combine to produce personal satisfaction.

Down with work!

Incentives and final goals are well worth thinking about. And perhaps we should take a long hard look at the attitude that work is somehow a good thing in its own right. It's worth examining, too, statements like 'Hard work never hurt anyone'. Rubbish! Hard work, whether physical labour or stressful mental work, can kill people. 'Work ennobles' is another pronouncement in a similar vein. Try telling that to Third World kids who labour in sweat shops. The Germans have the right idea about this one. They say 'If work ennobles, I'll stay a commoner'.

It's also said that if work were really the great thing it's cracked up to be, the rich would have kept it for themselves! Certainly 'working class' would never be used in a disparaging way, as it often is. In other words, work – in the words of the old joke – is 'the curse of the drinking classes' so perhaps we should avoid it at all costs.

We have to admit that a book designed to show *how winners win and losers lose*, especially in the workplace and which begins by advising people to work as little as possible needs a bit of explaining. The fact is that we firmly believe that in many cases *work is an activity undertaken reluctantly and which is fundamentally unpleasant.*

Fortunately, one person's work is another's fun and vice versa, so that travelling round the world might be sheer hell to one person and a constant delight for someone else. At the same time there are people who get a kick out of writing reports or balancing books.

This means that, if we are to be winners, it is immensely important to choose the right job, namely one in which the things we like doing – and which therefore cannot be considered 'work' – outweigh those things we don't particularly enjoy

If you think about it, it is obvious that some work will be enjoyable while other work will not:

Working for subsistence pay: Working to live, especially if the work is unpleasant, can be regarded as genuine work.

Working for 'good money': This is a grey area as far as work is concerned; already an element of 'play' is creeping in as we are working for pleasant things, like houses, cars, good clothes and holidays. However, if we hate every minute of it, it is still work.

Working for good money when you enjoy some of what you do: This is where we begin to be winners. The more we enjoy the activity for which we ultimately receive money, the less it deserves to be called 'work'.

Employment, whether on our own behalf or with others: The word 'employment' originally meant to implicate or involve, which is more of a winning approach. Of course, even in the best types of employment, we may find ourselves having to do some 'work' within the meaning of the Act.

It's a truism that not all jobs are the same and that some forms of employment offer more opportunity for enjoyment than others. However, all jobs provide some opportunity for gratification. Even slaves probably derived some enjoyment from their work. They certainly enjoyed singing work songs and one can imagine a day when the skies were blue and the sun warm, when the work seemed almost a way of beating time to the music and life seemed pretty good, if only for a moment. In fact, we could draw a graph with slavery at the bottom of the scale and total unadulterated enjoyment at the top, although the job that was all enjoyment would be pretty boring after a while.

Real winners get plenty of satisfaction out of their jobs – enough to allow them to enjoy going to work and to look forward to it – but at the same time, they experience enough challenge to make the job interesting without being stressful.

Losers can be winners

Sociologists have identified a tendency to promote people above their real capabilities – a situation which can cause the person concerned a great deal of stress and unhappiness. This is a good example of an apparent winner who is, nevertheless, a loser. If apparent winners can really be losers then apparent losers can be winners and in the situation mentioned above, for example, if there were two candidates for promotion, both equal in every respect, and one was promoted beyond his level of competence, then the candidate who missed out on promotion would be the real winner.

In other words, apparent losers can be winners, apparent winners can be losers.

Working to win

As we have noted, hard graft isn't always 'work' and you can keep busy at your job and still enjoy it! Of course, in order to be a winning situation, this sort of job should also be reasonably well paid. Job satisfaction is a bonus.

However, there are cases in which no money is involved and in which the effort required, over long periods of time, is enormous. A classic case is the Marathon for which thousands of men and women train hard for months and then run 26 miles, 385 yards, most with no intention of achieving personal financial gain. All the runners who complete the course – and most of those who don't – are regarded and regard themselves as 'winners' and derive enormous satisfaction merely from taking part. They would certainly not see the immense effort they put in as being work unwillingly undertaken. Once we discover what motivates people to make this tremendous effort, we will be able to use this form of motivation, together with all the other forms of non-financial incentives, to help us become winners.

Winning is contagious

As we've seen, winning is a habit, but it is also contagious. Join a winning team, even as an also ran, and you stand a very good chance of becoming a winner yourself. What we are seeking is the sort of super-incentive that in wartime persuades perfectly ordinary people to make tremendous sacrifices, put in colossal effort and take horrendous chances, up to and including risking their lives. We need to generate the sort of excitement which in wartime makes people claim that they have never felt so alive – but of course we need to do so in peace time. We need that champagne feeling in our lives, especially our working lives, that comes from being a winner.

Winning is sexy

Winners are sexy – motor racing champions, for example, are usually surrounded by bevies of beautiful girls and nowadays, female winners are sexy too – witness the last Olympics. In fact, there is a definite correlation between winning and sex – presumably with evolutionary importance. Perhaps for this reason, winning itself is sexy and winning at work, for example, can produce feelings akin to sexual gratification. Not everyone who goes to work knows this.

Winners and winning

Obviously, winning and losing are not always the straightforward issues they appear to be. As we've stressed, *everyone can be a winner*, but what constitutes a winner, how do you recognise a winner and, most important of all, how can *we* become winners?

Advice for new employees

1. Do more than just get by.
2. Train and be trained.
3. Take advantage of every opportunity.
4. Be fair to the company.
5. Seek solutions and not problems.
6. Enjoy your work – and smile.

Six golden rules that were given to every new recruit in one 'winning organisation'.

2

What Makes a Winner?

Playing 'Spot the Winner' is easy – after all, winners do tend to stand out from the crowd – but deciding what makes them winners and how we identify them isn't quite so simple.

One thing that complicates matters is that being one of life's winners or losers is a matter of degree so that we need to judge our own place and that of others on a scale of, say, one to ten, or draw a simple graph with total losers at the bottom and super-winners at the top. What we are aiming for is a position as close to the top of our winning scale as possible.

At this stage it might be useful to estimate your own point on the winners' scale. Just how much of a winner or a loser do you think you are? Then ask a friend to estimate your position. Don't lose sight of the fact that we are asking you to estimate your place on the graph *at the moment* because people, families, companies and even countries can change their position on the Winners' Scale dramatically.

Of course, if this were not the case there wouldn't be a lot of point in a book called Winners Win, but it is amazing how many losers believe that their place at the bottom of the scale is immutably fixed. Mind you, in the old days, there were a lot of people around who were only too happy to assert that this was the case and even to maintain that 'winners' and 'losers' were ordained by God. There are still a few such people around, but nowadays most of us realise that we can influence our place on the graph and the mere fact of reading this book is an acknowledgement of the possibility. *By accepting the possibility of winning, you have taken an important step towards becoming a winner.*

Of course, although today there is no question of our place on any scale being fixed for ever, there are still people who enjoy more advantages than others, having been born, for example, beautiful or rich, and while occasionally too much wealth or too much beauty can turn people into losers, in general terms neither could be realistically considered a handicap.

How much are you worth?

There's an old story about the chap who went to a psychiatrist to get help with what he thought was his inferiority complex only to be told, 'I'm terribly sorry but you really *are* inferior'. So are some people really worth less than others?

Curiously, many of us who suffer from low self-esteem would be hard pressed to come up with genuine evidence of our inferiority but, even so, it would be fatuous to claim that we are all equal in every respect. Obviously, some of us are taller, stronger, prettier, brainier and so on than others, just as some of us are born into wealthy families and some into poor ones.

Self-esteem is largely a matter of punching our weight and making the most of what we have. We are all different but we are all miracles and, far from making us inferior, our differences make us unique so that there is a case for stressing those things about ourselves which set us apart from other people and help us to become winners.

Even physical attributes which might be seen as drawbacks can sometimes be turned into advantages; for example, there are fat comedians – and for that matter comediennes – who base whole careers on being over-weight.

Mind you, you don't have to be a giant or a dwarf to make your appearance an integral part of your personality and a relatively minor physical characteristic like flaming red hair which makes some people's lives hell can be a boon to others.

Winners are the Greatest

It's not easy to assess the value we put on ourselves partly because it often varies from day to day – but it's easy enough in general terms to find out whether our self-esteem is high or low.

... Practical winning

How do you value yourself in relation to other people? Give yourself a mark on a scale of one to ten to indicate how clever you think you are. Assess in the same way how good-looking, attractive, efficient, likeable, fit, cooperative, assertive, etc. you think you are.

Now get your partner or an acquaintance to answer the same questions about you. If you can persuade them to answer the same set of questions about themselves it will help to ensure that they take the thing seriously. This is a straightforward simple quiz with no trick questions and if you consistently score under five the chances are that your self-esteem is too low.

If this is the case, what can be done about it? First of all you have to admit that like all human beings you are a pretty wonderful piece of machinery. Then look at any scores that were particularly low and decide what, if anything, can be done to improve them. Don't worry too much at this stage about the overall score because in the case of self-worth anything you do to improve your score in one field will automatically increase your score in most of the others.

Money, in fact, has never made people into automatic winners, but there was a time when whole sections of the population were divided into winners and losers on the basis of the particular stratum of society into which they were born.

The class system – winners and losers

The class system which attempts to divide people into classes ranging from lower class to upper class with any number of subdivisions in between is still with us but, fortunately, it is no longer as constricting as it once was. It must be difficult for people who were born after World War II to imagine the class system as it was, even between the wars, and TV shows like 'Upstairs Downstairs' gave only a vague idea of the real thing.

Today, many people find the terms 'upper class', 'working class' and so on objectionable but they are undeniably useful and, as the system effectively divided the whole population into winners and losers for centuries, it is worthwhile having a brief look at it to see how it operated and to find out what, if anything, we can learn from it.

The first thing we notice is that there were lower class winners just as there were upper class losers but they were considered rarities. In fact, there were probably a great deal more of both than was realised, but the interesting thing is that not only did the upper classes expect to be winners, but the lower classes almost without exception supported them in their expectations. Nor was this solely a question of wealth and position; a poor 'gentleman' – unless he was literally down at heel and often even then – would be usually treated with the utmost deference by members of the 'lower' classes.

The upper classes expected privileged treatment and almost always got it – which was quite a 'con' trick and one which worked for centuries. 'Confidence tricks' – in the criminal sense – are well named as they depend for much of their success on the confidence of the perpetrator and much the same applies in the social context.

The upper classes received – and to a certain extent still do receive – privileged treatment, largely because they had been brought up to expect it. Whole sections of society were trained to believe that they were 'winners' as of right, entitled to travel through life first-class and secure in the knowledge that even if they proved to be losers in some ways, they would lose within a supportive winning framework of family, friends, clubs, regiments and so on.

Families and schools combined to encourage them in this comforting belief and provided a whole package of recognition signals like old school ties and accents which announced to all and sundry 'Here is one of life's winners'.

In the Services they were expected to become officers and usually did, in which case their winning expectations and recognition symbols were formalised.

In the workplace, they expected to be selected as executive material and in many organisations they were considered the only possible choice for posts of any seniority.

Of course, many of them, whatever they themselves may have believed, were never total winners because they allowed themselves to become smug, self-satisfied, arrogant and selfish in a way that real winners do not.

Once you have spotted a patently upper class winner or two, look out for a classless or lower class winner. It's surprising how many attributes and qualities they share. Whatever the background, for instance, winners are confident, well groomed and well dressed in the sense that they are totally comfortable in whatever they happen to be wearing.

Winners attending formal dinners for example almost invariably look as though they were born wearing their evening dresses or dinner jackets, but will still be readily identifiable as winners while wearing overalls or fishing gear.

Spot the winner

Although most winners look the part, it is largely the winner's interactions with others that make him or her a winner, which means that winning is rarely a solitary occupation. In fact, winners are to be found almost everywhere and while it is important to be able to spot winners in the workplace, it is not always easy because their status as genuine winners can be obscured by hierarchical and other factors.

For instance, it is a little difficult at first to identify a senior executive as a loser when she is surrounded by the trappings we have come to associate with winning, like a large office, a company car, a secretary and so on. At the same time, it may be equally difficult to spot, say, a scaffolder as a winner who is poised, confident and happy.

This is why it's perhaps easier at first to spot winners in a social context where their winning status is not masked by position in the hierarchy. Try winner spotting in a crowded bar for example and you could well find that winners are served quickly without making a fuss while others who are shouting and brandishing notes or empty glasses are neglected. What's more, they seem to be able to manage this whether the person behind the bar is a blonde beauty, an old crone or for that matter a retired all-in wrestler, simply because they have a winning presence.

Of course, body language does come into it – winners don't hover uncertainly around the bar – but this is the natural consequence of their presence and their ability to project it.

Interestingly, the winner's ability to command good service is rarely resented by the other customers, even should he or she inadvertently be served 'out of turn', whereas they would have been furious had the same thing happened to a non-winner. This is the case not only in the social context, but in other environments including the workplace. In fact, it is worth noting that *real winners* are rarely resented.

Of course, being served reasonably quickly in a pub, while it may be desirable, is hardly vital but – as we shall see – *winning is habit forming* and a win in one area leads to wins in others. It's worth noting too that winners make getting good service appear effortless. Certainly they don't seem aware of having achieved anything remarkable because winning, in this sphere as in others, has become a habit.

Occasionally, even winners have to wait longer than they feel they should and this is where you will see winners shift gear, usually into the charm mode. 'A large gin and tonic please, when you have a moment' said firmly, but with a smile and without a hint of sarcasm, gives the essential information that the winner would like a drink, while 'please' makes it a polite request for help rather than an order and the 'when you have a moment' acknowledges that the person behind the bar is busy and at the same time establishes a suggestion of complicity.

The next thing to notice is that the winner anticipates a positive response and a confident expectation puts the winner well on the way to receiving it.

In a shop or pub, try to become invisible – in some places this shouldn't prove too difficult. Attempt not to be noticed by the staff and see how long it is before someone asks if they can help you.

Next try projecting yourself as a winner using only body language. We don't at this juncture mean jumping onto the counter – although there's little doubt that this would work in emergencies – but merely looking as though you expect to be served. Positive posture, eye contact and a confident smile all help. So does movement – because as snipers and hunters know, movement draws attention.

Then try using body language together with a typical winner's phrase when asking for service. If you feel less than totally confident, try using a tape recorder until you are satisfied you have hit the winning note before trying it out in a real life situation. This may sound contrived and manipulative, as will many examples of practical winning, but with practice, a winning tone and a winning turn of phrase will become totally natural. *Winners do manipulate people but they do so without malice … it's all a question of habit.*

Winners don't crawl

Real winners don't go in for boot licking mainly because they 'know' they have no superiors – only people who are positioned above them in the hierarchy of the job, the office, the army or whatever. They treat people in authority with respect but one way to identify them is that they are easy in their dealings with their seniors. Next time you are spotting winners in a social situation, watch out for the after-office-hours gathering which includes the boss and identify the winner or winners among the subordinates. They will be the ones who are treating the boss with relaxed informality as 'first among equals'.

'A winning boss is one who can operate his secretary's computer.'

Anon

Your choice

Now that we have had a chance to think about winners and losers we can make our own lists of winners and losers selected for example from royalty, politicians, athletes, stage, film, TV personalities and so on, including fictional characters. Is the Queen a winner for example? Surely the Queen Mother reaching her 101st birthday makes her a winner? And what about Prince Charles – he clearly hasn't won everything? Remember that we are assessing winners on a scale of one to ten and that we are looking for total winners – not merely people with a great deal of power or money. Bear in mind, too, that anybody can move up or down the winning scale and that yesterday's loser may be today's winner. For example, we might place Princess Anne a great deal higher on the scale today than she was a few years ago, but what do you think?

Next, assess your family, your friends and your colleagues, including the bosses, taking care to keep the lists in code or in a safe place. Mind you, we have only begun to look at the question of *How to be a Winner,* so keep all your lists and check them later on to see if your assessments have changed. Of course, the object of spotting winners at this stage is largely to pick up winning tips, which brings us back to practical winning.

Practical winners

When it comes to clothes, taste is more important than money. A genuine winner can walk out of an Oxfam Shop looking as though she has spent a fortune while a loser can spend lots of money and still look like a tramp.

Winners are usually able to pronounce foreign words – and for that matter English words – correctly. This is sometimes due to their background but more often than not to the fact that winners are self-confident and therefore not easily embarrassed, which means that they are never afraid to ask.

Winners and faux pas

Everyone, no matter how brilliant and sophisticated, is bound to put his or her foot in it every now and again. In fact, the only difference between winners and losers in this regard is that winners do not worry about faux pas, gaffes, solecisms or any other sort of booboo.

They prefer – as a matter of convenience – to be aware of such things as correct pronunciation and the conventions of polite behaviour but they lose no sleep over such trivia; self-confidence, humour and common-sense are all it takes.

... Practical winning

Make your own lists of characteristics which apply to winners and those which seem more appropriate to losers. You could start with the ones we've been looking at and then add any that have occurred to you while Winner Spotting. You may for example have noticed that *winners are attractive people* or that *winners are rarely envious.* We'll be looking at these and other winning characteristics later so hang on to your lists and add to them as we consider how to acquire the winning habit.

Strokes for the closest people

Love is a perfect example of a game for two players in which there should be no losers. In fact, it's a splendid example of a holistic win because, in terms of happiness and much else, the whole is greater than the sum of the two parts. Winners in love can expect a huge pay-off – but they should also expect that this relationship may be more fragile than many others.

Real strokes for close folks

People like to be complimented, which makes 'stroking' an important part of a winner's armoury. Partners and lovers not only respond well to verbal stroking but usually enjoy an affectionate hug into the bargain. Most men know, for instance, that women who cook for a partner like to be told that a particular meal was great, especially if they get a bit of a cuddle to go with the compliment, but only winning women seem to realise that their tough, hard breadwinner likes to be reassured every now and then in much the same way.

Even these days, women who have a career still take most of the responsibility for looking after the home and children. Winning partners, as well as helping, should be lavish in praise and appreciation. Burning resentment in one partner and lack of understanding in the other can destroy what might have been a winning team.

What makes a winning partnership?

Many of us expect too much from our partnerships and, since we frequently expect nothing less than perfection as our due, it's little wonder that we are so often disappointed. However, just as frequently, because we have no means of knowing what's waiting for us round the corner, we are likely to pitch some of our expectations too low so that we miss out on some of the potential win factors in our partnership.

A list of the elements people expect to find in a winning partnership would vary enormously according to their age and circumstances but it would be likely to include such desirable things as companionship, great sex, mutual assistance and a compatible sense of humour.

It would be less likely to include things like a verbal shorthand and body language amounting to a private communication system, or the reciprocal back-up which enables a member of the partnership to face the world as a member of a winning team, or the conviction that each of the partners would have at least one person on their side – no matter what they did.

Building up a winning 'us against the world' partnership takes time but at least, once you have mentioned the winning concept, you have opened up a dialogue, which is vital, and you could be well on the way to finding out what it would take to make your partner a winner.

At the same time, by making yourself a winner, you provide your partner – naturally without spelling it out – with both an example and an incentive.

Say, for example, that over the years you have become something of a careless slob. Now, as part of your campaign to become a winner, you could smarten yourself up and attempt to look better. It's odds on that if your partner too has let him- or herself go a bit, your lead will be followed, just as, if you open up a conversation on a topic of real interest to your partner, you stand a good chance of getting a reaction.

This may be simplistic but it is amazing how many people find it difficult to ask their partners, 'What sort of day did you have?' or, 'Shall we have a cup of coffee or would you rather have a gin and tonic?'

Great sex

Winning in bed is definitely important. For one thing it is a vital part of winning within the partnership and for another it illustrates, perhaps more than any other form of winning, the precept that *in order to win you don't have to make someone else a loser* and that, on the contrary, the way to become a winner is to make certain that the other person wins too.

It is also a good example of holistic winning in that the total satisfaction is greater than the sum of the two parts. Good manners, consideration and respect, together with a hint of humour, are more important than technique, while communication – especially when it develops into an exclusive 'language' – can be the most important thing of all. Above all, sex should be enjoyable for both parties. In sex, as in everything else, real winners assume they – and their partners – are going to win. There is nothing big-headed about this assumption which amounts merely to a mutual anticipation that all is going to go well.

Comfort zones

We might define 'comfort zone' as somewhere where you can feel totally at ease, non-pressured and in control of your self and your environment. There are several possibilities.

Your home should be a comfort zone – a retreat for bruised egos, a power base, a castle, a nest, a womb and lots more besides; a real home in fact. It should also be portable in that you ought to be able to take a lot of the comfort you derive from your home out into the world and especially into the workplace. Knowing that you have a supportive team at home, even if it is a team of one, makes all the difference to winning away. The trouble is that some people – often, but not always men – who find it tough to win at work, think they can win at home by being bullies and tyrants. Such people – usually members of the Jobsworth clan (who we will meet in detail later), are losers, because only losers would alienate their potential fans.

A comfort zone, not a cold comfort zone, is what winners should aim for because a winning home gives you a base from which you can conquer the world.

Cars are a splendid example of the mobile comfort zone. They are private space and, especially when used for driving to work, can be an extension of the home comfort zone or even a replacement for it.

Here, the lone driver, who may well have chosen the decor and furnishings of the car, also gets to choose the entertainment, the noise level, the temperature and air circulation. Being in charge of it, he or she can also move it at will, traffic permitting.

Some psychologists believe the car to be a symbol of sexual potency, but whatever, the car does place the driver in a position of power which makes it a good field in which to win.

Sadly, some people take this comfort zone/field in which to win to extreme lengths and believe that all other road users should treat their car/driver/space with all due deference. They may feel that they are winners, but, in reality, the aggravation and enmity they engender is counter-productive.

Mr Nice Guy

Getting up those few minutes earlier helps winners to leave a harmonious comfort zone behind them which makes them better able to cope with the frustrations of the road. Even these frustrations are eased by leaving a few minutes earlier because the pressure is off and it can prove possible on occasions to take a slightly longer route to avoid the worst of the traffic.

However, no matter which route you take, this could well be the first time since getting up in the morning that you come up against members of the Jobsworth clan. This sad, widespread family is represented in most grades of society so the mobile Jobsworth is as likely to be driving a top-of-the-range BMW as a tiny banger with nodding dogs or fluffy dice in the rear window. Their only distinguishing feature on the road is their incredibly bad judgement, and even worse manners, which is their way of countering a lifetime of losing frustration.

A highly satisfying way of countering the motorised Jobsworth is to drive with impeccable manners and near super-human consideration, especially as winners employing these tactics often seem to finish up in front anyway.

The workplace comfort zone

As we've seen, winners make their homes into comfort zones and if they travel to work by car they ensure that the vehicle is a movable comfort zone. The next step to becoming a holistic winner is to make certain that the workplace is a comfort zone.

Often physical comfort and well-being is the easiest to achieve and, in the spirit of holistic winning, will boost efforts to make the workplace a comfort zone in other respects. Individual winners build up their physical comfort zones in different ways but one obvious method is to personalise one's space.

Obviously, if you have your own office and complete control over its furnishings and decor, your workplace can become a winning tool as well as a comfort zone. It should reflect the winning personality you wish to project without being intimidating. Power decorating went out with Hitler – or should have done – so forget the long walk to your desk, the bright light shining in the face of your visitors, the uncomfortable chair or even the 'sink out of sight' armchair. Winners, who are all you want on your team, are up to such dodges anyway and can change most of them to suit themselves with a polite, 'Excuse me.'

If you have an office but not total control, you can personalise your environment and make it into a comfort zone by introducing a personal element, especially something from your home comfort zone like a favourite picture, flower vase, plant, china cup and saucer, or even a hat rack.

A comfort-zone desk

Many people nowadays work in open-plan offices where a desk is the only private space and anyone who wants to see how comfort zones evolve almost automatically should take a look at a new open-plan office after a couple of weeks of occupation and see how the screens, notice-boards, filing cabinets, pot plants and the like have appeared as if from nowhere to mark off personal or group comfort zones.

Most winners need only one item to personalise a desk comfort zone. We know one man for example who has an expensive-looking, gold ballpoint pen, in an equally impressive stand, which he says makes him feel and act like a winner every time he picks it up. Whether they have a palatial office or a battered metal-topped desk, winners who spend any amount of time sitting down should insist on a decent, well designed chair. A badly designed chair can not only make you feel like a loser but will almost certainly make you ill, and an employer who can't appreciate that sorting out this problem is an example of winning in which both sides gain and nobody loses should be regarded as a potential ex-employer.

Winners make friends

It's surprising how often even normally friendly folk seem to go out of their way to annoy people at work, especially those they consider to be lower in the scheme of things than themselves. Winners, on the other hand, without being either ingratiating or condescending, make friends at all levels through the organisation. Merely by being reasonably pleasant they are often able to get even the most crabby of Jobsworths on their side which, considering that the Jobsworth creed involves hating everyone, is quite a feat.

In fact, winners often find it surprisingly easy to get on with Jobsworths and to enlist them as willing members of their official – or unofficial – team, simply because they take them off guard by treating them as human beings, maybe even allowing them to recognise and operate in the winner's personal comfort zone – a winning and disarming trick.

Winners behave as if they own the organisation in so far as they are keen – if only for their own comfort – to have everything run efficiently and smoothly, and are prepared to input suggestions to save time, money and even paper clips. Setting one's own comfort zone at work is not just indulgence – it permits the best possible output, the most productive use of time and the least personal hassle. Winning bosses recognise this and stimulate it, so if your boss isn't interested or shows no enthusiasm for ideas, you could be in the wrong job.

Language

Winners make use of the fact that language is an important part of people's comfort zones. The special words used by lovers, partners and families, the jargon used by professionals, thieves' cant, slang and even languages themselves are comfort-zone accentuators but they do tend to result in 'them and us' situations, as when the Greeks called foreigners 'barbarians' because their unfathomable languages sounded like the noises made by sheep.

Winners know that learning a few words of a language – however exclusive – can help prevent them from being regarded as total strangers. Language can help win the objects of our desires, can make us into leaders, can frighten, arouse, hurt or hypnotise. Language (which differentiates us from animals) is an extremely powerful tool for good or evil, but it is not the exclusive property of any one class or person. Simplicity is one of the keynotes of winning language and two of the most winning words in any language are the simplest of all – 'please' and 'thanks'.

The people who forget these social niceties are the losers. However, words are also used elsewhere by the losers – and to devastating effect sometimes. Remember the last time you had a serious row with someone? You may have won the argument through the employment of biting, sarcastic, demeaning or otherwise crushing words, but you would not be deemed a winner within the constructs of this book.

In the home, perhaps as much as anywhere else, winners make their immediate surroundings into a conversational comfort zone for the whole group, but this does not mean that all conversations within the family have to be banal, colourless or even completely amicable. In fact, the home is the ideal place for winners to sharpen their conversational claws. Most animals learn to defend themselves by indulging in 'play' fights and though these can become fierce as the combatants become stronger and more experienced, few animals are seriously hurt. Winners take care to observe the effects of their words and back off when the signals are clear that enough is enough. Losers either cannot see these signals or choose to ignore them and perish by their own verbal hand, as it were.

... Practical winning

Winning words – Make your own list of winning words and phrases. Try to remember and note down occasions on which people have given you instructions in ways that have left you feeling (a) well-disposed towards them and happy to comply and (b) disgruntled rather than a winner. You could be surprised to discover how long the memory of how people spoke or wrote to you has lasted – a fact which emphasises how important winning words can be.

Winning words are usually the shortest and simplest that will convey exactly the meaning we intend, but this doesn't mean that winners can get by on the vocabulary of 800 words or so which make up 'Basic English'.

Winners can improve their vocabularies by osmosis, especially if they vary their reading material, but it speeds things up if they look up in a dictionary any words that are not defined by their context, after being encountered a couple of times.

A large vocabulary helps winners to understand what they read. It also helps them to understand what they hear, but it should not be used to make other people feel like losers. Again, if you want to have a laugh at people who use words incorrectly – especially if they are pompous idiots – it's a winning move to wait until you get home.

One way of building up a winning vocabulary is to make a note of derivations when you look up words as this will often enable you to acquire a whole family of words at a time.

Incidentally everyone, but everyone, no matter how brilliant or how well educated, makes a mistake with words every now and again, especially in conversation. Winners have the confidence to laugh at their own mistakes with words – and to learn from them.

Writing

Whilst talking about winning words, it is worth mentioning winning writing. Most winners enjoy writing – largely because, unlike most other forms of communication, it enables them to marshal their thoughts into a winning form before expressing them. They can get their brain into gear before sitting down at a computer and they know that, if they compose their message correctly, it will often have a greater and more permanent impact than the spoken word and that a written message is frequently the preliminary to a personal encounter and can set a winning tone for it.

Our two ideas of simplicity and compactness apply equally to writing but brevity doesn't imply rudeness. On the contrary, a short letter often requires more thought than a long one and is therefore a compliment to the recipient. As French philosopher Blaise Pascal put it, at the end of a long and rambling letter to a friend, 'I'm sorry to have troubled you with this long letter but I'm afraid I didn't have time to write a short one.'

A winning rule of thumb for notes and business letters is to try where possible to get all that you wish to say on to one page. If you need to introduce more than one important subject it is often worth writing several letters, which not only enables you to follow the 'keep it short', one-page rule, but also makes each of your subjects seem more important and therefore more likely to produce a winning response.

Keeping letters short also helps us to concentrate the mind on the message and to avoid, for example, needless repetition. Remember that the person whose attention you are trying to capture may well be extremely busy so it is no use burying your most important point in the middle of a load of verbiage.

Winners frequently use a three-part formula of (a) gaining attention, (b) explaining the situation, (c) suggesting action. Without implying for one moment that winners should ever be terse or rude, a note reading: 'You rat, you owe me £20 – pay up immediately!' would almost certainly produce better results than a ten-page letter.

Winning words can transform a piece of paper into an ambassador to another person's comfort zone, whether it is their home or their office, which could be one of the reasons why many people find junk mail an abuse of privilege. Of course, newly appointed ambassadors have to present their credentials and conduct themselves rather differently from those who have been in the same embassy for years. In the same way introductory letters and letters to people you don't know well have quite a different ring to those addressed to friends and long-time acquaintances.

Winners know that in most circumstances good manners and consideration for others are key factors in written communication, although there may be the rare occasion when winners feel obliged to use the written word to blast open a comfort zone and shock its inhabitants into action.

A final thought on words – business cards

A winning move with visiting or business cards is to buy the best you can afford. Keep them uncluttered and find out the local ground rules for their use. The Japanese, for example, have a whole business-card etiquette which requires, among other things, that in order to win, you must refrain from writing on the back of your card, which must also be handed over in such a way that the recipient can read it as it is being tendered.

Flying away

Building up comfort zones, by increasing our self-esteem, by making our partners and our families winners and by recruiting a winning team in the workplace, is an essential part of holistic winning. Unfortunately, ever since we were expelled from our first comfort zone after nine months or so of warm, safe, carefree existence, most of us have been a little reluctant to leave any substitute comfort zone we may have found.

This is why – although the term itself is useful – we prefer to regard the comfort zones as comfort 'bases' from which we can sally forth to conquer new and exciting worlds.

This doesn't mean that there is anything wrong with building up our bases – far from it – but only that remaining in the womb, however comfortable, is hardly a winning tactic. Birth is the real victory, and if later we build ourselves cocoons they should not be prisons but places in which we prepare for changes which will allow us to face a more interesting and challenging life.

We have looked at several comfort zones and shown how they can be used as bases when we begin to spread our wings but, in fact, leaving our comfort zones is an essential part of the winning process. Fortunately it is also, as a rule, something we are able to practise.

Winners know that it's only natural to feel a little apprehensive about the unknown and the unusual and go out of their way to overcome any fears they may have by deliberately moving out of their base. However, they appreciate that in the main such shifts up – or down – the social scale are best undertaken in gradual stages.

Becoming a social chameleon is a lot of fun and once again in the spirit of holistic winning there's a bonus. There are many jobs and professions, pastimes and interests where the ability to talk to people in all walks of life is an essential qualification and, even if your contacts are relatively limited, it pays to be at ease when talking either to the office boy or the managing director – and their equivalents in your social circles.

Obviously the ability to socialise at all levels can pay winning dividends and these are far from being limited to sharing a lift with the chairman or discussing the weather with the milkman.

Social skills of this sort enable us to leave our base in the home or the workplace and sally forth into other people's comfort zones and, here again, it is often a good idea to take this type of foray in easy stages – perhaps by, wherever possible, visiting or socialising with people in societies or departments that are similar to our own. However, after a while, winners should be at ease in every section of their environment, even those which are peopled mainly by those of the opposite sex or from different backgrounds – perhaps even both. This sort of winning, as much as any other, becomes a habit, so much so that, often in a remarkably short time, winners have built up a network of friends and acquaintances throughout their social world as well as the organisation in which they happen to be working. This can in itself lead to wider contacts and often makes life much easier as the winner moves upward and outward, encompassing more and more areas of interest and expertise.

Tip from the Top

'Dress for where you are going – and not where you've been.'

3

Getting the Winning Habit

As any gambler knows, being on a 'winning streak' is a magical experience, taking them into a world where they can do no wrong, where every card and every horse proves a winner, a world where the odds have no meaning and fortune favours the reckless.

Sportsmen too know the thrill of a winning streak, the rush of adrenaline and the iron-clad certainty that the vital serve will be an ace or the hazardous golf shot will end up on the green.

Winners – real winners rather than lucky gamblers or on-form sportsmen – always appear to be on a winning streak; they almost invariably get the job or the promotion, often without seeming to try. We call such people 'lucky'; folk wisdom recognises their existence as 'jammy bastards' and soldiers refer to them with affectionate envy as 'Mars Bar Experts' implying that if they fell into the latrine, they would surface clutching a well-wrapped chocolate bar.

Winners really do win

Winners really do seem to win more often than other people. It's almost as if they had a positive attraction for good fortune and, while a gambler's lucky streaks come and go, winners consistently achieve their aims in ways which make their wins appear inevitable. Of course, there is no denying the existence of luck, even though some things like good health or affluence may well be the result of sound planning by the 'lucky' person's forbears. However, this sort of inherited good fortune, while it may help give people a start, does not necessarily make them winners, any more than being dealt a reasonable hand ensures a win at cards.

Conversely, being born without inherited advantages doesn't automatically condemn a person to be a loser. In some cases, being born without 'advantages' can help make people winners by providing them with added incentives, although there is a danger that it may trigger off the sort of ruthless ambition which, while it may lead to material success, doesn't produce winners.

At the same time too many advantages can sometimes turn people into losers by making them idle, self-satisfied and inconsiderate. In fact, if you're ever tempted to envy people who were born with silver spoons in their mouths remember that some of them will never have the wit to find the bowl.

The rich man in his castle

Envying people who have been born with the sort of advantages we've been talking about is like envying the wind. It's the kind of envy that can give you ulcers, which is another reason why winners are rarely envious of anyone. It may seem unfair that some people get the chance to develop winning habits early on in life, but fortunately today almost anyone can become a winner.

There was a time, however, when God was thought to have decided in advance who was going to win and who to lose. In the words of the well-known hymn, 'The rich man in his castle, the poor man at the gate. He made them high and lowly, and ordered their estate.' What a load of Victorian codswallop! It was intended as an admonition to the poor to 'know their place' and a bit of Heavenly reassurance for the rich who at the time could still hear the echoes of the tumbril in every squeaky cart wheel, and it's the sort of nonsense with which winners will have nothing to do whatsoever.

Of course, we know that the 'poor' man might have been passing the rich man's gate on his way home to a loving family or carrying one of the rich man's pheasants under his coat. For that matter he could have been waiting at the gate with a hired chaise in which to spirit away the rich man's daughter while the rich man skulked in his castle worried sick at the thought of losing his money, his gamebirds or his precious little girl. If this were the case, the 'rich' man would be a loser while the 'poor' man would be a winner, so in this sense people's estates may well be 'ordered' in so far as their characters are predisposed towards happiness or misery.

However, this is not governed by position or material possessions and – once the basics have been catered for – there are so many different ways of winning that life provides prizes for everyone.

By basics we mean food, warmth and shelter because without those it is tough – though by no means impossible – to even think of becoming a winner. Given the basics we can begin to consider the sort of prizes we wish to win, remembering that *what other people tell us will make us happy may not in fact do so* – so there is obviously more to this business of winning than meets the eye.

Who wants to be a millionaire?

Well, you and me for a start – but, even so, there could be a difference between us because, while one of us is serious about becoming a millionaire and has done a lot towards achieving this aim, the other is still jogging along happily in the confident expectation that, one of these days, it will start to rain money.

All the contestants on Chris Tarrant's 2001 TV show wanted to be millionaires, as does every buyer of National Lottery tickets and the players in Littlewoods pools ... the opportunities to try are legion, even if the chances of succeeding are minuscule.

Still, most of us consider ourselves to be winners in one way or another – which brings us back to our definition of a winner as someone who is 'happy in his or her skin' and one of the secrets of attaining this sort of happiness is to get the winning habit.

As we've seen, people who have inherited wealth or position frequently become winners because they have been brought up to expect to win, which is all very well for them but what about the rest of us? Fortunately, it is almost as easy to acquire winning habits as it is to pick up bad ones and, by getting into the habit of winning, we can teach ourselves to expect success and how to project this expectation as a powerful positive force.

How do the 'lucky' ones do it?

What the silver spoon merchants are able to do from an early age is to exert a degree of control over their own lives. Even exercising partial options in such matters as choice of school, choice of sport, holidays and so on means that most middle class children have some degree of control over their lives and that this increases rapidly as they get older so that, by the time they reach university, they have acquired the winning habits which will last them as long as they live.

Conversely, some of those who are less fortunate may well find that they have lost control of whole areas of their lives, in many cases without even being aware of it.

Taking control of our own lives is the most important step in the process of becoming a winner. Of course, if you are dominated by bosses, subjugated by sales managers, crushed by customers, or even hen-pecked and harassed by your partner, the mere thought of taking control of your own life can sound ludicrous. How can you possibly take control of your own life if you are a salaries clerk with a dragon of an office manager, a secretary with a demanding and overbearing boss, a factory foreman with an autocratic works manager or a middle management executive with an MD who enjoys wielding the whip?

The most important win

The answer is to take control of those parts of our lives which we can control, beginning with those which cannot be controlled directly by others.

In fact, although it may sound daft, *the most important victory many of us will ever win may be accomplished simply by getting out of bed*. Mind you, it does entail getting out of bed a little earlier than usual but even that doesn't sound much of a win. Its importance lies partly in the fact that it could well be our first triumph since deciding to become a winner and partly in what we can call the knock-on effect. Say for example that, in order to get to work in time, we have to get up at 7.00 and that for several years we have been getting up at exactly that time because that is the very latest we can leave it – providing we rush our morning shower, gobble down our breakfast and are lucky with whatever form of transport we use to get us to the workplace on time. This means that – indirectly – our boss has begun to exercise control over us long before we even set off for work.

The trouble is that, whether we realise this to be the case or not, we feel this control and resent it in a way which can poison the whole of our day. However, the truth is that the boss *can't* exercise direct control over the time at which we get up. It is something which we control and – assuming that we don't wish to be late for work – our control can best be exercised by getting out of bed anything from a few minutes to an hour or so earlier than we have to. Getting up just ten minutes earlier, for instance, would allow time for a leisurely shower, a civilised breakfast and a quiet stroll to the bus, or whatever, instead of a mad dash.

... Practical winning

If you are one of those people who have timed the getting to work process to the nearest second, remind yourself of how it feels to get up feeling resentful and to rush through your morning ablutions losing a few seconds here and there when you are unable to find a new tube of toothpaste or whatever. You know the feeling; you can't lay your hands on the shirt or blouse you want and this leads to a slanging match with your nearest and dearest which wastes more time and leaves only a moment for a snatched cup of coffee, most of which you spill. Because of all this you miss the bus or hit a traffic jam and arrive at work in a filthy temper which is not improved when you realise that your pay has been docked or that you are the target of some barbed managerial sarcasm. Even if nothing worse happens – and it usually will – your day is shot, and perhaps your evening too.

Now try imagining – you can do it for real later – that you have got out of bed just fifteen minutes earlier than usual, which gives you time to appreciate the fact that it is a beautiful day as you peer out of the window before taking a shower, getting dressed and having a leisurely breakfast. Naturally, as you are not in your usual tearing hurry, everything you need is to hand and you leave the house – perhaps after a few moments discussion of mutual plans for the evening – in good time to stroll down to the bus stop with a friendly greeting to any friends and neighbours you may meet on the way. If you are driving, you are early enough to take a slightly longer, less busy route than usual, arriving in comfortable time to find a parking place, check out the notice board and so on.

A little change can make you look forward to getting up. Perhaps you are looking forward to trying a new shampoo, new bath soap, new deodorant, new lipstick, new hairspray. Perhaps you are looking forward to wearing a new tie, new blouse, new underclothes, new belt. It is amazing how little things mean a lot. A win is a win is a win.

Pre-planning

Plan approximately what you are going to wear the night before. And check it. Clean your shoes the night before. To make you feel really good, wear a flower in your buttonhole or a spray on your blouse. These little things cost very little money. You will enjoy buying them and look forward to using them.

Winners don't try to score points off people by making them feel like losers

Sadly, a situation which arises fairly frequently is one in which dominant personalities in executive positions devote a great deal of effort to scoring off other people, fondly imagining that by doing so they are proving that they are winners. They are, in fact, demonstrating that they are captaining a team of losers.

The aim of the genuine winner is to become a member of a winning team in a winning company, not a winner in a company full of losers.

Controlling your patch

Starting the day as a winner is easy enough and, once you get to work, the way to win is to remain in control of your life. Of course, the amount of control you can exercise will vary according to the organisation and your position. However, some degree of control is available to everyone.

Naturally, most of us have our own ideas about the way things are run in the company we work for but, while there are usually ways in a democratic society in which we can make our views felt, this is not normally a way in which we can become winners on a day-to-day basis.

As we've seen we can begin to win by getting up a few minutes earlier than usual and, at the workplace, we can begin to win by taking control of our own lives in minor matters like the arrangement of the space in which we work.

If we work in an office for example, our desk and filing cabinets can be chaotic, cheerfully cluttered, efficiently tidy or obsessively neat. In most cases the choice – within limits – is ours, but in the long run reasonable order and tidiness is going to make things easier for us and, as a spin-off, be more efficient for the company. In the first instance, we are concerned with the benefits to ourselves and this demonstrates a basic motivating factor in the process of becoming a winner, namely, enlightened self-interest.

- Tidy your own patch, and don't let others mess it up.
- Get yourself a good pen or pencil.
- Get a good personal organiser if you need one.
- Have your own notice board.
- Put up your own calendar. The most decorative isn't usually the most effective. Get one to suit you.
- Move tools, chairs, tables to suit you. Keep looking for small improvements.
- Drink good quality tea or coffee. Experiment with new brands.

... Practical winning

Make a list, for example, of all the things – apart from murder – that would make life at work more pleasant, more enjoyable, less frustrating and more efficient than it is at the moment. These could include such things as getting a decent cup of coffee, obtaining a parking space, or submitting your expenses on time. However, if your list of possible wins includes getting the office grouch to smile it could be an idea to leave the list at home.

A good deed a day keeps losing at bay

We aren't suggesting that potential winners should get measured for haloes but merely thinking about what good deed you could do each day that could alter the way you think about the job and your colleagues. If, for example, you are a clerical officer whose supervisor gets totally pissed off about one of your minor foibles, like leaving papers strewn over your desk when you go for lunch, try doing things their way for a change. If people think things are important they are important to them, which means you can make them feel like winners without too much effort or sacrifice.

Real winners aren't usually calculating about such things, but, of course, casting bread on the waters is a good way of ensuring a supply of fish. If your subordinate has, for example, a wedding anniversary or for that matter a golf date, suggest they leave a few minutes early.

Blessed are the peacemakers but they do tend to get clobbered, so perhaps refraining from adding fuel to any fires that may be smouldering in the workplace should count as a good deed. People should feel happier and more like winners for having come into contact with you during the working day and this, of course, does you no harm at all.

4

The Personal Touch

Like most animals, people love to be stroked, but unfortunately nowadays – especially in the context of the workplace – physical stroking could be misinterpreted, so in most cases we have to confine ourselves to verbal stroking and other less intimate gestures of appreciation. Mind you, it does seem a shame that – in Britain at any rate – we have all but abandoned this useful form of communication, along with the rest of the contact gestures, so that we miss out on the genuine comfort of 'a shoulder to cry on' or the pleasant glow that we once derived from a real 'pat on the back'.

People in other countries are much more demonstrative and to become a winner on an international scale, you should at least be aware of the local customs in this respect. As far as the British are concerned, shaking hands seems to be one of the few contact gestures left to us. For the moment, since the handshake is pretty much our only physical contact method of initial signalling, it pays to get it right. This should be absolutely self-evident but it is amazing how many people – especially men – condemn themselves as losers within the first seconds of meeting someone for the first time by using horror handshakes.

- Horror handshake number one is the macho maul or death grip, designed to leave the other person writhing in agony and often used by male executive losers to establish what they fondly imagine to be dominance. Some men habitually use this grip on women, presumably to demonstrate which is the stronger sex, and although winners do not approve of violence as a rule, female winners might find a high heel applied firmly to the offender's instep suitably discouraging.
- Horror handshake number two is the limp lettuce effect, often combined with damp palms, and totally self-defeating. This is sometimes made even more unpleasant by a total reluctance to let go, in which case it becomes the politician's linger.
- This is exceeded in unpleasantness only by the pseudo-sexy (sometimes two-handed) handshake offered by some male executives to female subordinates, which is a really tacky abuse of authority.

… Practical winning

Winning handshakes should be firm but gentle and should last not much more than a second. They were originally intended to show that you had no weapon in your right hand or concealed up your right sleeve. They should still convey much the same message today, which means that wet palms are out and that, for anyone who has naturally sweaty hands, surreptitious drying is in order.

Practise handshakes – they really are that important – first of all by shaking your own hand, then those of friends of both sexes. Do the whole bit, combining your handshake with a friendly smile and greeting. Imagine different scenarios for your handshake. Meeting your new boss for the first time, meeting new neighbours at a party, experiencing love at first sight in a splendid nightclub and so on.

Don't worry if you feel a bit silly at first. We wouldn't like to take bets on it but we wouldn't be surprised if more contracts, business and social, weren't won or lost on a first handshake, than because of any other single factor. Winners create a good impression and your handshake can help you do just that.

Find a good book on dealing with different cultural approaches to greetings, handshakes and the like. Do not assume that the often informal way you can meet British people will be matched by the expected way to greet Germans of Finns. Their cultures may demand a different style and you ignore that at your peril. Likewise, different cultures have different 'personal space' – the physical space surrounding each person that cannot be invaded. Winners will know how close they can get (or not) and how enveloping the greeting can be. Watch the wide range of embraces and greetings from formal, swift handshakes to whole-body hugs when guests arrive to meet the 'victim;' on *This Is Your Life* programmes, for instance.

Sex in the workplace

Winners don't go in for 'sexy' handshakes, but both male and female winners use sex to help them win in the workplace and elsewhere. They'd be mugs if they didn't – and winners are not likely to neglect anything which could give them a winning edge.

This does *not* mean that winners are forever trying to 'score', especially in the workplace – far from it. It doesn't even mean that they 'come on strong', as our American friends have it, with every member of the opposite sex they meet. As we shall see, there is a correlation between winning and enjoying a successful love life, but for the most part, especially in the workplace, the winner is content to use sexual interaction on a low key level to attain such mundane advantages as a decent cup of coffee, access to a senior executive or a couple of minutes extra on the lunch break.

Winners use sex in this way almost without being aware that they are doing so and to a genuine winner, using the mysterious spark of sexual appraisal and approval, communicated in a glance or a subtle change of voice timbre, is all part of the stroking process. It makes the other person feel good; in fact it can make two people feel like real winners for the whole day – even though they may hardly have said much more to each other than 'Good Morning!'

For a novel and fascinating analysis of the way men and women interact at work, see *The Yin and Yang of Business Communication* by Laurel Alexander, Management Books 2000, 2001.

Winners see people

It is fairly easy to 'stroke' a person of the opposite sex by recognising their existence as a human being, especially if they are reasonably attractive, but sometimes it is not so easy with people of the same sex. Bosses – even very minor bosses – often drift into the habit of treating their subordinates as if they didn't exist as people. By contrast, winners see everyone as a person and have a smile and a word for everyone, without, however, being so aggressively cheerful as to get on people's nerves.

Winners do tend to smile a lot – or people who smile tend to win a lot – so smiling is one winning habit to acquire as soon as possible. For one thing it helps you to feel a winner but, more importantly, it makes the people you meet feel like winners too. In fact, smiling is so important that some large organisations have run whole campaigns aimed at teaching their staff to smile.

This doesn't mean that winners should go around with inane grins on their faces – only that it's a good idea to greet people with a smile and to smile at fairly frequent intervals while you are talking to them.

After a while, smiling becomes second nature, but because smiling is easy, don't knock it. It's an essential weapon in the winner's armoury. In fact, being able to smile naturally is a real help when it comes to acquiring the natural good manners that all winners need. Of course, we are not talking here about the sort of 'manners' you might learn at a school of etiquette. A winner's good manners are considerate rather than formal so they can be acquired merely by taking a conscious decision to treat other people as you would wish to be treated yourself. 'Do as you would be done by!' doesn't apply only to children.

It costs nothing to be polite

When it comes to winning, the *magic words* are 'please' and 'thank you' and the *magic phrase* is 'I wonder if you could help me.'

Saving one second by giving a brusque order rather than making a polite request is counter-productive, especially if the person concerned then spends several minutes complaining about your bad manners to a colleague. As for the magic phrase 'I wonder if you could help me?', few people can resist a request for help because it flatters them and gives them a chance to demonstrate their knowledge or expertise. Again, don't overdo it, but on the other hand don't struggle along without help that you need, just for the sake of asking.

A golden rule of conversation is to remember that most human beings, whatever their age, race, creed or social status, are convinced that they are the most fascinating creatures on earth and that their activities, relationships, politics, illnesses and so on, past, present and future, are the only topics of conversation which are of any real interest.

... Practical winning

How many times did you use the magic words today?

For practical winning, begin by using these words more often than before, especially in the workplace and in service situations like garages or shops. This may seem elementary, but so many of us are under such pressure in today's world that we respond by using a sort of verbal shorthand which cuts out all the grace notes like 'please' and 'thank you' which, though it may appear efficient at first sight, sounds like rank bad manners to others and could prevent us from becoming winners.

Sell yourself – but softly

Winning, as we hope we are making clear, does have a great deal to do with selling ourselves and many of the attributes of the genuine winners are those we recognise in first-class salespeople. In fact, there is no harm at all in reading a good book or two on selling style in the quest for winning pointers, provided we beware those sales manuals which teach salespeople to regard their prospects as mug 'punters'. Winners never treat other people as 'mugs', but always as winners or potential winners – after all, who wants to deal with a loser?

Like really good salespeople, winners know people's names – or have worked out useful ploys like 'Oh! I know your first name of course, it's your second name I've forgotten,' or vice versa – because they realise that people's names are among their most prized attributes.

It is virtually impossible to remember the names of more than two people when you are introduced for the first time. Awkward introductions at a party are a classic case. It is extremely difficult and embarrassing when a host introduces you to a group. You will have a winning chance if you know some of the names before you arrive. It is much easier to put faces to names than names to faces.

Find out who is going to be at the gathering and write down and memorise the names before arriving. Also find out the first names as well as the surnames. It is much easier to remember Nick Thornely rather than J. N. Thornely. It is easier to remember first names as they sometimes give you a clue to character. Sue, Pandora, Mary, Johnny, Sam, Walter all give you some picture in your mind. This practice will help you remember the name. Remembering people's names will give you a great feeling of achievement and this is a winning characteristic.

When writing to people, there is never any excuse for spelling their name wrongly. To spell someone's name wrongly is a losing characteristic. If you have already received a letter, then the signature is a vital clue as it has never been known for anyone to spell his or her own name wrongly. The telephone directory is a good source too as printing errors are very rare.

Most Americans are much better than the British at remembering names, but tend to be obsessive about repeating them. A couple of repetitions should enable you to remember a name and it does help if you are discussing the person with a third party to refer to him as Fred Bloggs from Wrigglethorpe's and not as Whosit from Whatsit's.

Keeping business cards of people you meet can be a winning move, but try not to finish up with a pocket full of meaningless cards. This can happen easily at parties – oh yes, it can! – so try to scribble a couple of words on the back of the card to remind you of the person and the circumstances. However, if you write something like 'pompous prat' on the back of someone's card, be careful to keep it safely hidden!

Incidentally, if you have an interesting or unusual name, make the most of it. Find out if it is Norman French, Viking, Serbo Croatian or whatever because that can make your name memorable and a memorable name can help to make you a winner.

It's what you know about who you know

Remembering names is only one way of 'stroking' and, of course, people feel even more like winners if you can remember what they do and a few other things about them, like their partner's name, what the kids are doing and so on. It may seem calculating but since even some winners have terrible memories, an extended contacts book can be very useful. In fact, we should think in terms of preparing a winner's contacts book with notes on the people we meet – including people who work for us on a casual service basis – with not only the basic details, but also a listing of their likes and dislikes.

Most of us don't even have available all the information we need about our friends and relations and while business directories like Yellow Pages or Talking Pages can be immensely useful, the sort of thing a winner finds it worthwhile to know about, say, the mechanic who did such a great job on the family car is that he's a darts fanatic or dab hand at French cuisine.

Getting on well with people is a real help when it comes to being a winner and, once you have made a good start at the first encounter, it's a shame to waste it for the sake of making a couple of notes.

Contacts in the workplace

If contacts in the social context are important, they are doubly so in the workplace where what people do is often considered to be more important than what they are.

Winners don't necessarily agree with this and their business contacts book should reflect this by containing not only 'name, rank and number' but a certain amount of personal information. Don't try to collect all the information at once, unless of course it is volunteered, and fill in the entries in your contacts book as soon after the meeting as possible.

... Practical winning

Lay out a contacts book with appropriate columns to include not only such items as name, address, occupation, title, phone number but also wife's name, children's names, birthdays, hobbies, affiliations, clubs, politics, not forgetting to leave space for comments like 'knowledgeable about computers' or 'wife runs cooking school'.

If you think making notes of this sort is 'sneaky' you may be interested to know that the Queen uses a very similar system – with a little help from her staff – and that people who are presented to her are often amazed and flattered to discover how much she knows about them, especially if she has met them on a previous occasion. This is stroking of a very high order and it works. More about this later.

Compliments

Remembering people's names and a few details about them, although absolutely essential, is a very elementary form of stroking compared to the delicate art of the compliment. People love compliments and are willing to believe almost anything good about themselves but as most winners realise instinctively, in the end insincere compliments can be counter-productive. People love to be complimented on things like their dress, their appearance or their possessions and a winner should be able to use a genuine compliment to take the sting out of criticism.

For example, a secretary who tells the office boy whose whistling is preventing her from getting on with her work, 'My! Henry – you do sound cheerful this morning,' is going to stand a better chance of persuading him to stop, than if she had said something like, 'For God's sake, will you cut out that racket.' Praise should be genuine and the winner's motto should be 'If you can't praise, at least don't knock.'

Receiving a compliment

Many people are confused and embarrassed to be on the receiving end of a compliment. People blush, stammer and have even been known to contradict the giver of the compliment. There is a simple response which is always pleasing and acceptable. If someone says, 'You're looking good today,' just smile and say, 'Thank you.' Why argue? Enjoy the feeling of being a winner.

Praise in the workplace

In the workplace, as elsewhere, too much praise tends to debase the coinage but, if you have people working for you, you could find something on which to compliment them, even a small thing, once every day. Encouragement in the morning followed by praise in the afternoon is good winning strategy. It's much better to send people home smiling than scowling because the impression they take away from work, whether good or bad, is going to last – and perhaps grow.

You could also find that in looking for something for which to praise people you discover that you really have got a winning team working for you which can only make you more of a winner. Everyone loves a genuine compliment and winners use them to leave other people feeling like winners even if they have to criticise something. 'I like the way you've set that out – but . . .' is a typical winner's solution to the problem of telling people you think they are wrong. So get the compliment habit – but remember, it's like watering plants – essential, but it's a mistake to overdo it.

Stroking the boss

Complimenting people who hold higher positions in the workplace can be tricky because there's the obvious risk that you could be suspected, whether by the boss or your colleagues, of being a creep, which is definitely not the attribute of a winner. This is unfortunate because it puts many people off saying anything remotely pleasant to their boss which means that they could lose ideal opportunities to make the boss feel a winner.

Any compliments you pay to the boss should be absolutely genuine and, if anything, a shade less frequent than those paid to other people in your department. Most bosses like to be complimented on their business expertise, their successes and even their acquisitions – which they like to feel they deserve – so your stroking will normally be welcome. However, if your boss seems too remote for that sort of compliment, he or she would be unlikely to be upset by an oblique compliment like, 'I wish I had your magic touch with clients' – always providing it's true.

... Practical winning

Different strokes for different folks, as they say – but you might care to begin by verbally stroking your partner, if you have one, always remembering that to be effective, compliments must be sincere. 'That was a delicious meal' or for that matter, 'a really good bit of positive driving' could lead to a home win – often the most valuable of wins. As we have seen, there are 'different strokes for different folks', but there are not many people who don't respond well to the knowledge that they and their efforts are appreciated.

After practising stroking on your nearest and dearest – your partners, parents or siblings – move on to compliment colleagues and see how it helps turn you, and them, into winners. Note too how, if you have not been given to appreciative comments in the past, a few words of praise will usually cause the person concerned to try even harder. Of course, your praise should be sincere, so practice looking for things to praise and you could soon find yourself a winner – in a family of winners.

Tip from the Top

'You never get a second chance to make a good first impression.'

5

Winners Can't Be Losers

Winning is a cumulative affair – so much so that it is often difficult to decide which came first, the winning chicken or the prize egg – and this is one reason why it is so important to get the winning habit, to start winning in small things, to achieve minor goals and reach intermediate targets. Once you get the winning ball rolling, it is like a snowball on a hill covered in soft snow, small at first but gradually becoming larger as it picks up more snow until it becomes huge and unstoppable.

At the same time winners begin to behave like winners in their dealings with other people and, once again, it's a little difficult to tell after a while whether they are behaving in a courteous and considerate fashion because they are winners or whether it is the way they behave to other people that makes them winners. The answer, we believe, is that the real winner – the sort of winner we are talking about in this book – is a holistic winner, a complete winning personality to whom winning comes as naturally as breathing. He doesn't have to think about whether he is going to be polite or considerate to people in the workplace, for instance, because knowing he is a winner gives him unshakeable confidence *even when things go wrong.*

The confidence trick

Once you have played the game of spot the winner a couple of times – especially in the workplace – it's easy to see that winners are confident and unafraid while losers tend to be fearful. Not that winners go around talking tough to the boss for example: quite the opposite in fact. They are as polite to the boss as they are to everyone else. It's merely that they know they could be tough if the occasion arose – and so does everyone else. The remarkable thing is how little time it takes, once you have decided to become a winner, to acquire this special sort of confidence which, of course, marks you out as a winner and helps you win even more.

The secret lies in what the military experts call the **worst possible scenario**. As we shall see, motivation specialists use a different term for the Worst Possible Scenario and for what they see as the Best Possible Scenario, but for the moment let's stick with the WPS which, as its name implies, refers to the very worst that could happen in any given situation and incorporates Sod's Law which states: 'Anything which can go wrong will go wrong.'

Obviously, winners' confidence derives in part from the fact that they are good at their job, which they enjoy because it is just at the right level to stretch them without causing them stress and because they are well liked by their colleagues and their bosses.

However, this doesn't completely explain the impression they give of being completely impervious to the slings and arrows of commercial politics and industrial misfortune. In fact, their confidence is largely due to the fact that they have already examined the worst possible scenarios and faced up to the worst that could happen to them in their present situation. They have also made contingency plans, however tenuous, to deal with such situations should they ever arise.

... Practical winning

Worst possible scenario – try working out your own list of WPSs. Make a list of total disasters you might conceivably have to face, beginning with dreadful happenings in the workplace. Don't worry about grading them at the moment – you can place them in order of sheer horror later on. Of course, everyone's list will be different, but there will be a few common factors like losing one's source of income. One person's list might look something like this:

- The organisation goes bankrupt.
- I am fired.
- My boss leaves and I cannot work for the new one.
- The organisation is taken over and one of the jobs to go is mine.

These are all serious and often very real sources of anxiety, but if you examine them it's obvious that they are all fundamentally the *same worry*, namely that you are going to lose your job. Now winners, by definition, are less likely to lose their jobs than non-winners but, of course, they could do so. They don't think, 'it could never happen to me.' However, winners – while certainly not worriers – do practise worst scenario management which means that instead of concerning themselves with *four* unpleasant possibilities, some of which they can do very little about, they concern themselves with only one major disaster, i.e. the possibility that they may lose their job.

For the sake of convenience we may refer to this as **Worry Management** and, as it can save a lot of sleepless nights – not to mention ulcers – it is a definite step towards becoming a winner.

With only one disaster to think about, the winner can set about making plans to cope with it, which in this case – once you have taken all possible steps not to lose your job – means making sure that you have a parachute..

Winners have parachutes

Winners, of course, are less likely to be fired than losers anyway because they will have made many friends in their own organisation and outside it. Their friends inside their own organisation may not be able to help them keep the job they hold at the moment but they could, particularly if the organisation is a large one, suggest and perhaps implement a sideways or even temporarily downwards move.

Parachute 1

Prepare a CV and keep it up to date. It's wonderful how much more of a winner you will sound when you know it's only in fun, but it will be there if ever you need it. In the same way, keep a list of firms in your own line of work and write a couple of draft letters of application. Once again, when it's in fun you'll find you come over as the winner you are. However, don't leave the draft letters lying around! If the worst happens, you'll be very fortunate, even as a winner, to walk into a new job straight away, especially the exact job you want. Winners, of course, do tend to walk into better jobs than the ones they have lost but, while you can hope for this to happen, you can't count on it and it makes sense to think of short term solutions.

Parachute 2

If you were to be offered a different job in your present organisation, decide which jobs you could do and would enjoy and, consequently, which you would be prepared to accept – perhaps even on a temporary basis. Winners tend to have good contacts in other organisations similar to their own which they built up by friendliness, fair dealing and, let's face it, by keeping up with the gossip which, being winners, they are well placed to do.

Parachute 3

Make a list of contacts in organisations similar to your own, together with office and home phone numbers where appropriate. A little gentle sounding out might not come amiss and winners can strike just the right note of ever-so-slightly-serious banter with this one. Winners have their ears to the ground and are less likely to be caught out on any given 'Night of the Long Envelopes' but these things can happen quickly and it's as well to be prepared.

Parachute 4

Think of a temporary job you could do while looking around. A commission-only selling job is a good bet in this respect as it brings in money quickly which prevents reserves becoming exhausted and, as salespeople usually make their own hours, leaves you free to tackle the job situation in your own field without pressure. We are talking about direct selling here: if you can knock on somebody's door and sell them something, you need never worry about losing your job again and that alone puts you well on the way to being a winner.

Most winners can sell – most really good salespeople are winners anyway – so selling is an extremely useful parachute, so much so that it is a skill worth acquiring. If you have a daytime job which leaves you with your evenings and perhaps weekends free, take a part-time selling job for a month or so. Nowadays there is very little cold canvassing. Salespeople are given 'qualified' leads to prospects who have expressed interest in the product or service on offer and most firms will provide some training. Proving that you can sell not only provides a parachute – as well as paying for a new car or a holiday – but also makes you more of a winner in the workplace in as much as it is a great boost to one's confidence, enabling the winner to extend a purely imaginary two-fingered salute in the direction of the organisation's resident Himmler.

Selling of course is not the only alternative income parachute.

Parachute 5

Make a list of jobs you could do at a pinch, ranging from fairly down-to-earth occupations like tele-sales, temping or working in a shop to driving a lorry or becoming a dustman. Don't worry if some of the jobs you think of seem a bit lowly or off-beat. If the jobs are available and you can do them, it does mean that you and your family are unlikely to starve. Starving is, after all, what you are really worrying about when you worry about losing your job – starving and being without a roof over your head – but in fact the worst that could happen is that your lifestyle might be altered dramatically. In fact, living on very little money is not too difficult and can be something of a challenge provided that you have enough for basics and, most importantly, provided that the situation is temporary and that you *know* things are going to get better.

Parachute 6

Make a plan for living on the absolute minimum possible amount of money, distinguishing carefully between what you *want* and what you *really need*. Think in terms of selling assets – remember this is all hypothetical. You could, for instance, manage with a smaller house but would perhaps need to keep your car – if it belongs to you – for use in a new job or for transport to help you find a new position. In this connection it might be worthwhile, if you can afford it, to buy a reasonable 'old banger' as a second car, to reduce the trauma should you lose the company car.

List any other 'parachutes' that may occur to you. For example, if your partner is not currently employed, you could discuss the possibility of him or her taking a job for a while, should you lose your position. Partners should usually be involved in the Worst Possible Scenario planning from the start and obviously well before there is any chance of the WPS being realised. When it is all a game rather than a reality, both of you may come up with ideas for unusual 'parachutes' like turning what is now a hobby into a paying proposition.

Having dealt with a major worry, winners can use the Worst Possible Scenario technique to deal with most of life's disquieting features both in the workplace and at home. It is surprising how many worries vanish completely, for example, when you apply the principles of Worry Management, one of which is not to worry about things you cannot possibly do anything about, such as the earth being destroyed by a runaway comet. If you think that's silly, by the way, try making a list of your illogical worries of the week – and then stop worrying about them.

Winners do not worry too much because they have made contingency plans. Winners can afford to be independent, confident and fearless and therefore are less likely to lose their jobs in the first place. It's the chicken and the egg question again, but who cares which comes first – being a winner or winning – when all that really matters is that *winners rarely lose.*

Going for that new job …

Interviews are not the most pleasant of experiences, but committed winners can and do generally perform better than others.

Think winning

Because they have prepared themselves in advance, winners are unlikely to panic when faced with the real interview, but there are one or two things worth considering.

Winners, for example, think ahead. They have already imagined themselves doing the job for which they are being interviewed and this – without their being conscious of it – gives their approach confidence. It even changes their choice of words so that instead of, 'If I get the job, would I be required to …?' they might say, 'Would my responsibilities include …?'

Another reason winners do not panic is that they have convinced themselves of an important truth, namely that if – by some incredible stroke of misfortune – they do not get the job, they are unlikely to be taken out and shot. *To a winner, a disappointment is not the same thing as a tragedy.*

Some winners do suffer from nerves. After all, many winning actors still get stage fright even after years in the theatre and claim it helps their performance. Interviews, whichever side of the table you are on, are a performance, but if you do feel nervous, provided you are certain that you won't dissolve into helpless mirth, try to imagine the interviewers sitting there naked.

Both sides want to win

The most important thing to remember is that unless the job has already gone to the chairman's niece or nephew, the interviewers want to win for themselves and their company. This makes it highly unlikely that they have decided to waste an hour or so of their time at immense cost to their company in making the applicants look idiots. It's much more likely that they wish to finish the day with a warm winning glow and the chance to report to their superiors that, after interviewing some excellent candidates, they have come up with someone who seems ideal for the job. A good win-win situation.

Winning on the day

Winners are relaxed. As holistic winners, they are aware of their own value, their membership of a winning team at home and the fact that they have a comfort zone to return to – whatever happens.

They have prepared themselves by role-playing and are psychologically prepared for a *meeting* rather than a contest.

As winners, they have selected – and tried on – the outfit they are wearing, which is of course appropriate and comfortable, and they are clean, neat and looking good. One distinctive – but not garish – item of clothing or jewellery is permissible. It will enable the interviewers to identify you immediately when it comes to their post-interview inquest.

Because they look good, feel good and are well prepared, winners walk into interviews with confidence. Their posture is good and their speech clear and direct. Winners remember that they are applicants not supplicants.

Whilst waiting to be seen, winners do not sit down – you will be in a less winning posture if you have to peer up at the person inviting you in to meet the panel.

Body language should reflect relaxed alertness, not tension – no folded arms, for instance. You have something to sell to people you know are in the market and as a winner you are certain you have a great product. The interviewers' attitude can tell you quite a lot about the company. You are entitled to expect politeness from the panel, a preliminary effort to put you at ease and, eventually, a chance to put questions to the interviewers. Winners stress what they will be able to do for the company but they also want to know what the company will do for them. This doesn't mean, however, that your very first question should be about the company car.

Winners leave interviewers with the impression that they have found the right person for the job – someone who is prepared to make a real contribution, who puts job satisfaction and scope for eventual advancement high on the priority list and who will fit into the team.

6

What If the Jelly Hits the Fan?

There's nothing quite like being a winner and nothing to beat the bubbly, on-the-top-of-the-world feeling we get when everything's going our way, but what happens to winners when disaster strikes and brings hard times for individuals, companies or even for whole nations?

Can being a winner really help when we are faced with things like bullying bosses, conniving colleagues, slumps, redundancies and plain bad luck? Can winners still win when the jelly hits the fan?

The answer, of course, is that winning is always better than losing and that the same qualities which enable winners to be happy and successful, when things are going well, will usually make it possible for them to win when the world turns sour and even if things should go catastrophically wrong.

For winners, winning is a habit which is hard to break – even at the worst of times. Mind you, the winners we are talking about are not the win-at-any-cost, devil-take-the-hindmost type of people who trample everyone else underfoot in their desperate rush to be first, but the all-round, holistic winners who are happy in their skin and whose methods of winning help other people to become winners rather than turn them into discontented losers.

They are the winners who have made their homes and their workplaces into comfort zones, which include other people rather than excluding them and encourage them to form winning teams. Like almost everyone, such winners may well be motivated by self-interest but, in their case, it is enlightened self-interest of the sort which presupposes, for example, that should hard times come along it is better to have friends and allies than to be surrounded by enemies. Because of this, they will tend to be good negotiators whose aim is to find a 'win-win' solution to any confrontation in which both parties gain and no one loses. Theirs is the language of the draw and the bargain rather than that of total victory on the one side and unconditional surrender on the other and, though they are quite capable of defending themselves and others, they would almost always rather talk than fight.

This sort of person is easier to recognise than to describe but typical winners will have a good physical posture and a pleasant but forceful personality which, together with well-developed 'people' skills, will usually mean that they become the natural leader of any group in which they may find themselves. Largely because of their ability to get on with other people, they will normally have stable and happy family or social lives as well as being involved and successful in the workplace, whatever their status.

Winners sometimes appear to inhabit a different world from other people – a world in which there are fewer bastards, fewer shambles and fewer instances of rank bad luck.

In fact, winners live in the same world as the rest of us, an imperfect world full of villainous men in black hats, obstructive Jobsworths and devious types whose idea of humour is to let someone win the ship's lottery on the Titanic.

It's merely that winners are usually better able to cope with the world because they are able both to modify it slightly and prepare for its vicissitudes.

Shit happens (as Americans are wont to say)

Accepting the fact that disasters can happen – and that they can provoke other disasters, the effects of which are cumulative – is the objective and winning way in which to think of bad luck. Like the snowball which, if allowed to roll, grows until it starts an avalanche, disasters can often be stopped in their tracks, provided we are physically and mentally strong enough to act quickly and effectively.

When disaster strikes, apportioning blame is the name of the game and, although winners try to avoid the knee-jerk reaction of blaming everything and everyone they can think of, it is essential to determine the origins of each particular piece of misfortune as quickly as possible as this will almost certainly affect the way we react.

Some disasters, for instance, are patently 'Acts of God', genuine pieces of misfortune or bad luck, sometimes impossible to avoid, often seemingly capricious and unfair.

However, it is all too easy to regard our misfortunes as the result of bad luck, and when things go wrong we should almost always ask ourselves whether the fault lies 'not in our stars but in ourselves...' Of course, unless we are extremely lucky – and here again winners are more fortunate than most – some of the bad things that happen to us will be caused deliberately, unintentionally or perhaps unthinkingly by other people but, especially in the workplace where blame can bounce off the walls at the drop of a production quota, it's essential to ask whether we ourselves may not be at fault.

Again, some disasters really do have dark and complicated origins and there really are such things as plots and conspiracies, evil-minded bosses and colleagues, faithless, greedy and ruthless partners. However, when disasters appear to have complex or sinister origins like conspiracy or sabotage, it is often as well to ask if the real cause may not be something relatively simple rather than the World War III scenario we conjured up first.

Back to comfort zones for a minute

In good times, turning our homes into comfort zones provides winners with a base from which to win in the outside world. Winners leave such homes well fed, well dressed and full of confidence, knowing that they have at least one fan rooting for them and maybe more, as well as one very interested adviser and sounding board with whom they can discuss the day's events and celebrate minor wins and major victories. They are also in a good position to inaugurate the rest of the 'take PAINS' sequence (see page 78) by planning to avoid disasters and insure against them.

When times are normal, winners who have managed to make their immediate workplace 'family' into a comfort zone, and have good working arrangements with other such zones within their organisation on a 'customer relations' basis, will have a more harmonious and enjoyable working life. They will also have helped to make their organisation a great deal more efficient than those made up of mutually antagonistic loners in which most interdepartmental contact is viewed as an intrusion. Like members of home comfort zones, the workplace family will be in a good posture and will have gained experience in working together, often perhaps under pressure, all of which is excellent practice should disaster strike either the individual or the working community.

Communication is the keynote in creating home and workplace comfort zones and in establishing relations between the two. Many companies now recognise the importance of this interaction and encourage it by forming social and sports clubs, or in some cases by means of things like health care, insurance, creches and counselling services – all of which act as 'official' comfort zones. The creation of these is dictated by enlightened self-interest as they are intended to protect the workforce from the effects of worry and disaster, thus making them both loyal and efficient.

In this connection it is interesting that some of the oldest and most successful industrial companies like Cadbury's, W and HO Wills and Fry's were making their complete enterprises into comfort zones as early as Victorian times, not only by paying fair wages, awarding decent pensions and inaugurating training schemes, but also by providing good housing, canteens, clubs and sports facilities for the whole of the workforce.

When things go wrong at home

When things go wrong at home, the family comfort zone should provide mutual aid and consolation together with a refuge and a base from which to fight back. Those struck by personal disaster who are at the same time members of a workplace comfort zone should expect sympathy, encouragement and help from their colleagues in addition to any official aid. In the case of a major tragedy like a bereavement, for example, the workplace family can be expected to rally round with both sympathy and practical help like temporarily covering for the bereaved person, providing transport and assistance in dealing with probate and so on. The workplace comfort zone will also be of help in the case of minor mishaps from breakdowns to break-ups and will often provide a sympathetic hearing – or at least a hearing – for the occasional therapeutic moan.

When things go wrong at work

When things go wrong at work, the comfort zone of the workplace family is there to provide help and encouragement while closing ranks almost automatically if the disaster threatens from outside the group. At the same time, those affected by disasters in the workplace can expect to find sympathy, encouragement and practical help in their home comfort zones.

Beating the bastards

There's an old saying which goes '*nihil illigitimae carborundum*' or 'don't let the bastards grind you down!' which is excellent winning advice always provided you have correctly identified the illegitimates in question.

Unfortunately, bastards do really come in all shapes and sizes ranging from the Jobsworths – whose family tree often has a hint of the bar sinister – to the thorough-going copper-bottomed bastards with a short 'a' in the first syllable.

As we've seen, winners frequently succeed in recruiting run-of-the-mill Jobsworths to their official or unofficial teams but

Jobsworths who have a yellow belt in bastardy can be trickier to deal with. Linguistic judo on the lines of 'You're absolutely right about that, but …' can often be helpful with these low-grade illegitimates, and even those in positions of some authority, as can the implication that the winner is a member or the leader of a winning team as in, 'We think we ought to …' Often a winner's attitude – derived from a winning sense of inner worth, a winning partnership and a winning home base – is enough to defeat these minor villains.

Coping

The ways in which we can cope with disasters and their effects depend on what sort of disaster we are faced with and whether we are taking action before, during or after the event.

Sadly, even for winners, there is no magic wand which will enable us to win against all of life's possible mishaps, but there are ways in which we can organise both our preparations and our counter-measures in order to give us the best chance of winning and, to the extent that they can be expressed as a simple and near-universal sequence of recommendations, they are as close to a magic formula for dealing with disaster as we are likely to get.

The formula

Among the measures we can take before the sky falls in are the adoption of a winning POSTURE, the AVOIDANCE of disaster wherever possible and INSURANCE against its occurring.

Then, if and when disaster does strike, we must ASSESS the damage, COUNTER it, and where possible take action to TERMINATE its causes and prevent any secondary disasters it may provoke. In other words our main concerns before the sky falls in should be:

Posture
Avoidance … and
INSurance

while during or after the event they should be:

Assessment
Countermeasures ... and
Termination.

This means that the winning way in which to deal with disasters is to take PAINS to prepare for them, in case they should happen, and to ACT swiftly and efficiently if they do happen.

PAINS ☆ DISASTER ☆ ACT

Of course it is impossible to predict exactly what sort of disaster we may encounter, or when it will occur, which makes taking PAINS seem a rather imprecise way of dealing with disaster compared with ACTing in response to a specific piece of misfortune.

In fact, we have to be prepared for almost anything to happen at any time, and fortunately this is where winners enjoy a tremendous advantage in that, being winners, they are in a better POSTURE than most people to cope with disaster, whatever form it should take. As winners they are not only in better shape, both physically and mentally to face any difficulty that comes along but they are also well placed to overcome it, since they will already have made many winning dispositions like creating comfort zones, and will be confident of their ability to win whatever the circumstances.

In many cases, the winner's confident posture alone is enough to resolve the crisis and winners, for example, stand a much better chance than losers of obtaining a crucial bank loan simply because they look and behave as though they expect to win.

Again, in the course of becoming winners, especially in the workplace, they will have built up an informal intelligence network which will often help them to AVOID disaster or at least some of its effects. As for INSURANCE, the comfort zones that winners create at home and at work will help to mitigate the effects of many disasters. This is especially the case where winners have succeeded in making their intimate workplace 'family' into a comfort zone and where this zone has been expanded to ensure good 'customer relations' within the organisation as well as outside it.

Of course, in order to be effective in both good times and bad, comfort zones have to be efficient as well as happy. This means that winners have to be careful not to allow comfort zones to become complacency zones although, in practice, teams of happy winners who are enjoying their work will always be more productive than groups of discontented or terrorised people.

... Practical winning

There is a major 'disaster' in your home or workplace. Describe – using the 'take PAINS before and ACT afterwards' formula as a guide – how, as a winner, you would be in a better position than many other people both when the emergency arose and afterwards.

For example: there is a potentially calamitous disruption in the supply of vital components to your factory. As a winner you are in a good POSTURE to make some confident sounding phone calls. You will have made arrangements to AVOID the worst effects of such a disruption, while your INSURANCE in the form of good relations enables you to rally your own team and to call for help from other users of the same components. ASSESSING the damage is easy because of your information network which also helps ensure that you get honest answers to queries – and along with the efforts of your winning team will help COUNTER the effects by, say, getting hold of replacement components, while you TERMINATE the cause of the disaster by ensuring future supplies and prevent any secondary troubles by, say, placating those of your customers who may be affected by any delay in deliveries.

Winners won't fight

Winners won't fight – unless it's absolutely necessary. Like the man in the white hat in the classic Western movies, winners would rather talk than rush into a confrontation.

Winners, for example, will always explore the possibility that there has been a misunderstanding. There's always the chance that the other person is behaving like a bastard because he thinks – wrongly – that he has been cheated, badly done by, made to look small or otherwise affronted. A great many battles in the workplace – and even in social situations – can be avoided by winners saying something like, 'I'm sorry – we seem to have got off on the wrong foot. Let's get together over a drink and see if we can't make a fresh start.'

Winners can fight

The French have a splendid expression for wimps and pushovers; they call them *poires* or pears – meaning the fat, mushy variety you can poke your finger through.

Winners, of course, are not *poires*; they prefer not to fight but they can fight better than most if they have to and, while they may feel obliged to allow their adversary the first strike, they will rarely turn the other cheek. Like the man in the white hat, winners try hard to find another way before buckling on their guns but, like the good guy in the movies, when they do so they invariably have the advantage of surprise. Winners don't even raise their voices most of the time so that, when they do, people tend to listen.

Winners laugh in the face of adversity

An old Punch cartoon showed a young subaltern transfixed by a Zulu assegai, replying dryly when asked if it hurt, 'Only when I laugh.' In fact, disaster of some sort provides the raw material for most of the world's jokes and, although we tend to laugh louder and longer at the mishaps which befall other people than at the genuine catastrophes by which we ourselves are struck down, humour can be an important constituent of our winning posture, especially when things go wrong. Laughter can help a great deal in relieving tension both in individuals and groups and, when telling jokes, comedians make use of this by building up tension as much as they can, before suddenly releasing it with a punchline that triggers off laughter.

In worrying times, when tension becomes unbearable, winners are often able to make use of humour to release tension and thus avoid the build-up of stress which might otherwise feed on itself to the point where it became a medical condition. In much the same way, winners are able to use humour to relieve group tension and even to diffuse tense situations which might otherwise impair the efficiency of the group or even destroy it.

In good times, those of us who have partners or families are often able to practise this type of group humour until it becomes second nature and an integral part of the comfort zone, a code of 'family jokes' which becomes doubly effective in times of trouble. In the workplace, private jokes among 'family' teams fulfil the same function and the same group humour which helps give the team its cohesion when things are going well will help it to survive and win when things go wrong.

When things do go wrong, humour of this sort is often the best way to begin looking at our worries objectively but, although winners usually laugh a lot, they tend to laugh at themselves more often than at others and are careful not to use humour to turn people into losers.

Team humour, provided it does not involve a scapegoat, is often a good way of strengthening a comfort zone under adverse conditions. However, although the ability to 'see the funny side' of misfortune is a precious gift which many winners take for granted, and one which can lessen the effects of all but the most dreadful disasters, it is not a gift which is given to everyone and, when disaster strikes in the workplace for example, even winners have sometimes to be careful not to laugh themselves out of a job.

Winners can cry

Very high up on the scale of disaster – so high that many people given the choice would choose to die themselves rather than experience it – is the death of a loved one, a disaster that most of us have to face in the course of a lifetime. Like death itself, this is one of those few cases in which – although winners are in a better posture to cope and to fight back – it is difficult to think in terms of 'winning'.

However, winners, besides being in as good a shape as possible both mentally and physically to face up to hammer blows of this sort, may well have accepted the fact that the people they love are mortal – as they themselves are. They may even have considered some of the effects of such a loss on a Worst Possible Scenario basis but this can only lessen the shock by a fraction. What we are left with is grief – a complex emotion in which genuine sadness for the departed is often mixed with 'why wasn't I nicer to them' guilt and 'how could they leave me like this' self-interest.

It is an emotion which Anglo-Saxons do not always handle well and while, for example, the stiff upper lip may be an admirable trait when confronting life's minor upsets, it can't compare with clothes tearing, ashes wearing, weeping and wailing, or even for that matter a good wake, when it comes to the therapy which grief demands.

In this instance, people with firm religious convictions are doubly fortunate, as they have not only the comfort of their beliefs but the consolation of funeral rites in which the words, the solemn music, the eulogy and even the funeral meal all have a part to play in provoking healing emotions. Fortunately most churches recognise this as a humanitarian function and are prepared to help non-practising members and even non-members of their faith in times of bereavement.

Whatever provokes the tears, winners do cry when faced with this particular disaster, in order that mourning may give place to memories and leave the bereaved to get on with the business of winning which, fortunately perhaps, usually involves coping with any number of lesser problems.

Winners hate harassment

What is totally abhorrent to any winner is sexual blackmail or harassment in any guise and whichever sex is doing the harassing. Winners can usually prevent this sort of thing from starting by promoting the right atmosphere and by recruiting in advance allies who will be useful in this sort of emergency.

Winners try to nip in the bud any tendency among potential harassers to 'see how far they can go' because if they are allowed to continue, things can only get worse. Acting early can prevent the sort of persistent nastiness which makes life uncomfortable – even unbearable – and which can be more difficult to counter than physical harassment for which there is now legal redress.

Unfortunately, real life is not a Western movie and there are occasions when the bad guys are too numerous, or too powerful, to beat, in which case the only winning move is to leave town – although, of course – winners being human – it is often possible to 'dynamite' the place before riding out.

Winners bounce back

One characteristic all winners share is the ability to bounce back when their world has crumbled around them and to rebuild their lives – often better than before.

Whether they lose their money or their business, are struck down by dreadful illness or fail at the very moment of completing some cherished enterprise, winners will pick themselves up and – often within a remarkably short period of time – will be well on the way to another success.

Often their second major endeavour bears little or no relation to their original enterprise but, remarkably, their success will usually be at the same level. In material terms, for example, a millionaire winner on whom the sky falls may lose all his money but when he builds up a new business he will not usually make himself merely comfortable or even wealthy. He will be on his way to a new million – and almost certainly more.

This ability to bounce back is due in part to the holistic winner's conviction of his own worth and his wins in areas not affected by the collapse of the sky. However, the main reason is that winning is not only cumulative but habit-forming, so that winners become accustomed to winning, at whatever level they operate, and will usually go back to winning at that level even after a serious reverse.

One fine example of this is heavyweight boxer Frank Bruno who in spite of putting up a courageous showing, was defeated by Mike Tyson. Years later, Frank, who interestingly never lost his winner's status in the eyes of the public, was still thinking about whether or not he will ever put on the gloves in earnest again. Meanwhile he embarked on a new and successful career as an actor and TV personality and has managed to turn what was once regarded as an unfortunate speech habit into an instantly recognisable trade mark – 'Know what I mean, Harry?'

Winners use maps

There are very few new disasters, which means that whatever happens to us will nearly always have happened to someone before us and, as winners readily seek help wherever they can get it, they will be prepared to learn from people who have been through a similar experience to the one they may be facing.

That's why it is strange that so many of us elect to go it alone, repeating the mistakes of previous generations, and often those of much more recent forerunners, because we are too proud, too stubborn and too impatient to learn from others or to seek their advice.

Of course, this isn't always easy. Most of the younger people in the developed countries, for instance, seem to have been brought up to treat their elders with contempt – amused contempt with luck – which makes it hard for them to turn to parents or grandparents for advice when faced with potential or actual disaster, even though their older relatives may have experienced similar troubles.

In much the same way, in the workplace, new brooms are often in such a hurry to sweep clean that they brush away years of experience without learning anything from either the triumphs or the disasters of their predecessors.

It doesn't really matter whether the previous incumbent of the job has retired with honour and a gold watch or been ignominiously deposed; in either case it is worth making an effort to learn from people who may have experienced similar problems to those we shall be facing. In fact it is a shame to waste experience of this sort and, as we shall see, some progressive major companies have now introduced schemes specifically designed to exploit the know-how of their older employees.

Of course, it is not necessary to follow slavishly the advice of either older relatives or the person who had our job before we did, but winners realise that in both cases consulting and involving older or more experienced people is a doubly winning move. It can often help us to win by enabling us to choose a course of action when problems arise and it also gives those we consult a chance to win by making them feel useful and valued individuals.

Some worries are good for us

It's obvious from all the above that a few worries – as opposed to worrying – can be good for us, provided we are able to regard them as problems capable of solution because, in contrast to the strangling effects of worrying, problem solving adds interest and challenge to life, especially in the workplace, which might otherwise become dull and boring.

Looked at in this way, a worry – once we have decided that it is not the end of the world – becomes the irritating grain of sand in the oyster which can be turned into a pearl when dealt with correctly and adequately.

Of course, merely converting an irritating worry into a problem will not produce a 'pearl', but, as opposed to sterile worrying, it does help a great deal and, in fact, as with many winning moves, there are several important bonuses to the problem-solving approach.

The first is that – as we have noticed with regard to winning in general – solving problems is habit forming, so that over a period the divergence between worriers and problem solvers grows steadily more pronounced. At the same time, the effects of worrying, and conversely of problem solving which we noted above, are multiplied so that while life becomes, for example, even more stressful for the worrier it becomes proportionately less so for the problem solver.

A further bonus is that, while a worry, which vanishes spontaneously after having driven the worrier half insane, is likely to reappear at anytime with exactly the same consequences, the problem-solving approach usually provides us with a blueprint for dealing with any similar worry in the future.

At the same time, the process of problem solving itself can be so stimulating that occasionally it produces a bonus in the shape of a coruscating, mind-boggling new idea which, especially at work, could prove to be 'a pearl of great price'.

This is it!

The sky has fallen in. Disaster has struck – and this time the grave-faced policemen are knocking at *your* door, this time it's *you* sitting in an upstairs room waiting for a boat to rescue you from the flood waters or watching helplessly as firemen try to save your home. Maybe it's you people will see on the television news staggering away from a wrecked aircraft or reading the notice telling you that your organisation has had to close. Or perhaps your disaster is a more lonely one announced by a serious-faced doctor or a tearful partner.

Wherever disaster strikes, and no matter in what form, it is too late to plan, to prepare, or to insure. The jelly has hit the fan and now is the time to ACT; but first of all there is an intermediate stage which no one can predict or control, the time of immediate reaction to disaster, during which all of us behave differently but when winners behave better than most.

In any disaster, whether expected or not, there is always a specific moment when the policeman calls, the bomb explodes or when the figures can no longer be made to lie. For winners this moment of truth is the one in which their efforts to achieve a winning posture get their first test. This is the moment of **disaster shock**.

Fortunately, not only do many of us behave a lot better when confronted with disaster than we might have imagined but nature provides its own anaesthetic to cope with the most serious physical or mental wounds, in the form of shock itself. This means that while we may suffer acutely from minor wounds, or from relatively insignificant disasters like an unfavourable assessment at work, shock will help to preserve us from the initial effects of real tragedy and catastrophe.

Shock will soften the blow, through the first moments of disbelief and painful half acceptance, to the time of full acknowledgement of what has happened – which is when winners begin to ACT.

Winners and shock

A time when heroes – and cowards – are revealed. This is the time when, in the case of disasters like train crashes or natural catastrophes, heroes – and cowards – are revealed and people perform acts of bravery often without being aware of what they have done.

Very soon after this initial shock, winners begin to realise the advantages of their winning posture and most of them, for example, because of their physical fitness and mental resilience, will react more quickly than most to save both themselves and others, as well as being among the first to begin functioning almost normally after those disasters which leave others behaving like zombies.

Sometimes the fact that they have actively considered a particular disaster and its effects, as part of their taking PAINS preparation, will help them to begin behaving normally more quickly than others.

Assessing the scale of the disaster

The need to assess, as soon as possible, the extent of large-scale physical disasters is obvious. At a personal level, damage assessment usually involves taking an objective view of any given disaster and positioning it on a scale of nought for gnat bite to ten for terminal.

Winners, of course, will have the advantage of having considered in theory the gravity of many potential disasters but, once the worst has happened, the exercise must now be performed for real. This is when winners begin to appreciate that whatever has happened to them is not 'the end of the world' and that in many cases just being alive constitutes a considerable victory. We know several people, for example, who have survived life-threatening illnesses and who now consider every new day to be a 'win'.

Act to win

Once the first shock is over, assessing the effects of a disaster can itself be a form of therapy, forcing us to use our hands and our brains and pushing us in the direction of more positive action. However, making such assessments calls for honesty and, if we are to win through, it is no use trying to fool ourselves by fudging the facts or figures.

Writing things down often makes it easier to be objective and the first list to be made is one showing the full extent of the disaster and its effects – with the immediate effects in one column and the long-term effects in another.

Tip from the Top

'Every problem is an opportunity.'

7

Planning to Win

If you aim to win, it's as well to have a plan. It's no use thinking in a vague sort of way of winning 'one of these days'. This is one of the besetting sins of many people who look as if they ought to be winners, but who are still 'coming men' when they collect their gold watches.

The fact is that, no matter what sort of person you are, it does pay to have a plan but remember, *a plan is a plan* – just that and no more. It is not an immutable timetable, deviation from which will render the planner liable to be struck by thunderbolts. A rigid schedule which makes no allowance for changing circumstances or the vagaries of other people is as constricting as a strait-jacket and is something with which no winner would wish to be associated.

Winners make lots of plans before deciding on one they think should be feasible and, partly because they have considered lots of plans before deciding on a course of action, they are ready – and able – to change plans if need be.

Winners do daydream

More heresy, but winners do daydream and so they should. What winners do *not* do is daydream all the time. Daydreaming is constructive – it allows a part of your brain to come into play which is not used at other times and which may come up with some brilliant ideas. One way to get the best out of daydreaming and at the same time avoid being hooked on it immoderately is to set aside times and places for the exercise and to refrain if possible from daydreaming at other times. Some people find the bath an ideal place for daydreaming and certainly the tub has a useful reputation when it comes to generating ideas. Other people find that the few minutes before they drift off to sleep is a good time, but this does have disadvantages as it is quite possible to wake up next morning remembering only that you had a marvellous idea, but without the slightest recollection of what it was. In fact, it's not a bad idea, even in the bath, to daydream with a notebook and pencil to hand.

Germans call daydreams '*wunschtraüme*' or 'wish dreams' and this is exactly what winners' daydreams should be, because it implies that you can guide them in a specific direction. Daydreams, and especially those of the *wunschtraüme* variety, are really the first steps in planning. They are a game of 'How nice it would be if ...' and in the first instance, the only restriction to your dreams is the scope of your imagination, though for most people there is an undercurrent of logic in their daydreaming which is not always present in dreaming proper, so that daydreams hover on the fringe of the possible.

Dreaming how pleasant it would be to have our wishes come true is the first step in planning to make them come true. The next step occurs while still in the daydreaming mode, as vague plans begin to emerge, some of which may well be absolute nonsense. Kidnapping the Chairman at gunpoint for example is not perhaps the best way to go about getting a raise or even a parking spot in the organisation's car park. However, as you continue to daydream, you may stumble on a plan which is much less ludicrous and perhaps even several such plans.

Making dreams come true

Daydreaming, even constructive daydreaming, is not enough by itself and we now need to take a good look at some of the plans we have come up with while our minds were relaxed. It's not a bad idea to examine even the most bizarre, way-out ideas in the cold light of the office in case there is the germ of a real plan lurking amongst the wild schemes. Then pick the plan you like best and work through it on paper taking care to map out several intermediate stages.

Now take this plan – call it Plan A if you want to be original – back to the daydreaming stage to see if your subconscious will come up with any further inspiration. At no stage should you totally reject Plans B, C, D etc. because they could come in handy later on. Winners do change horses in midstream if the horse they are riding weakens.

Most winners do this sort of pre-planning without even being aware of it. If you have never used the daydreaming part of your mind, you are missing out on a valuable weapon in the winner's armoury but don't worry, it is an easy skill to acquire.

It is now time for us to bring our conscious minds into play and one of the best ways of moving from the daydreaming mode to the conscious mode is to write things down. This is not to say that we shouldn't make notes of any bright ideas we derive from our daydreams; of course we should, and the sooner the better, but in the planning mode writing things down becomes much more purposeful.

What do you want to achieve?

You have now had time to sort out your dreams and to decide what it is that you really want and what you feel will make you a winner. You have also had the opportunity to engage in *wish management* – much the same way as we tackled worry management – by grouping our wishes together where appropriate and by deciding which major wish is achievable.

For instance, if we wish for a new house, a new car or a diamond necklace, what we are really wishing for is more money; if we wish to be admired, respected, loved, to have more friends at work and out of it, what we are really wishing for is more personal success.

Winners work in three stages

We have talked about dreaming and that is an essential start. Alas, 83% of the population never get past the dreaming part. To make dreams come true, there is actually a proven system to make it happen.

- the dream ↳
  - the desire ↳
    - the determination

Dream

The first step is to write the dream down.

Winners write things down

This system is frequently called 'Goal Setting', but it doesn't matter what you call it as long as you do it. The 83% of the population who don't set goals are the losers. They don't set goals for various reasons. Firstly it requires effort, and that puts people off. Secondly, the fear of failure overrides the excitement of winning. Thirdly, you are certain to be ridiculed by friends, colleagues and loved ones.

I'm certain that Wilbur and Orville Wright were ridiculed by just about everyone, particularly friends and loved ones. 'You mean you're going to fly in that contraption. Fly in the sky!'

Winners write down their goals whether they are major goals (like the Wright brothers) or more modest goals. They write them down in the present tense. Yes, the present tense.

In order to do this, it means you must actually be able to visualise the achievement of the goal some time in the future. The more vivid this is, the more likely it is to happen. There is no point is saying, 'I want to lose weight.' There is no point in saying, 'I want to be rich.'

Writing the goal requires careful thought and time. A good way to write your goal is to write these three words first:

> 'I am enjoying ...'

So, if one of your goals is to lose weight, your goal might be:

> 'I am enjoying looking at the bathroom scales on Christmas Day and seeing 65 kilos as my new weight.'

You can feel the difference between the two weight-loss statements. One is a wish list, and the second one has purpose, energy and excitement.

Financial security is another. Instead of saying, 'I want to be rich,' which is a wish list, try writing:

> 'I am enjoying receiving my Bank Statement because it will show that I have £... in my account.'

If one of your wishes is to move to a better and bigger house, your goal might look like:

> 'We are enjoying the house-warming party at our new house.'

It can take a while before you get the wording right for your goal. Persevere so that when you look at the written goal, you feel a sense of excitement every time you see it. In fact, you should look at your goal many times a day, and perhaps even paste it in a conspicuous place. Near your workplace or next to your bathroom mirror.

Desire – winners are selfish

The definition of **Desire** is 'an unsatisfied longing or craving'. Thus the goal has to be something you feel very strongly indeed. That is why you have to think of yourself. Think of me!

Having written your goal, and displayed it somewhere you can see it many times a day, remember that winners usually write down selfish reasons why they want what they want.

While you are doing this, you will feel a power of ownership. You will also quickly realise there are benefits to others when you achieve that goal. They could be loved ones, friends, colleagues, the environment, and even the country. The selfish desire comes first.

Most winners keep this list of selfish reasons in secret. But keep it in a place where you can refer to it immediately when your plans and goals run into problems, which they will. Those desires need to be strong.

The Dream and The Desire are all important to motivate yourself to get going. They are the vital ingredients. Winners write down their goals. Losers think it is embarrassing and trivial to write things down, and they are probably too lazy. That is why losers are in the 83% of the population.

The surprising fact is that *it is not very difficult*. The first time you try it, don't be too ambitious, but it will demonstrate to yourself that there is a system and you can use it over and over again.

It is not difficult to be a Winner, but you will have to step away from the crowd and do the things that Losers don't do.

Determination

This is the hard part, but again there is a system. Achieving the goal becomes part of your daily planning process. On your 'To-Do' list make certain there is some task or action that is helping you on your way, every day.

Many winners use the Priority Matrix from Stephen Covey's best-selling book *The Seven Habits of Highly Effective People.*

The two key elements on all the tasks on your 'To-Do' list are:

- How Important is it?
- What is the timescale?

It is likely that many of the tasks or activities related to achieving your goals are 'Very Important' but not 'Very Urgent'. These are classified in the Priority Matrix as Quadrant 2.

Priority Matrix

	Very important	Not important
Very urgent	1	3
Not urgent	2	4

Winners get the important tasks done. They are good at planning, delegating and communicating.

The beauty of having a 'To-Do' list is that you are winning every time you complete a task. Just crossing it off the list gives you that winning feeling.

Losers feel that making 'To-Do' lists is a waste of time. Losers imagine that they have fantastic memories.

Winners know that their memories will let them down sooner or later, so they don't take chances.

Write it down and forget about it.
Ink it when you think it.

Losers think it is boring to be well organised with lists, diaries, address books and so on. Winners know that it is essential.

... Practical winning

The winner's Bible – the contacts book. We've talked about lists of contacts but now is the time to start a contacts book – not merely an address book but a real contacts book – with all the pertinent information about the people we meet, and maybe even a bit of gossip. If you don't already have a suitable book, buy a good one that's meant to last and with lots of space. Make sure you write down the name and address of every new contact you make plus a short identifying note and cross references where appropriate, for example:

Bloggs, Fred (address, phone number) sales rep for Papertrade PLC – keen gardener – wife social worker – good man to deal with.

When people give you their business cards, make a note on the back of each one as soon as you can saying where you met and any relevant information not on the card, for example, 'John's party – int. in buying car' or 'Club – could be client.' Do not write 'Met in Bull's Head – wimp.' By all means note people's less pleasing characteristics where relevant but, when you do so, use a simple – and deniable – personal code.

As we mentioned, making this sort of note, especially on the cards you pick up on social occasions, will save you from finishing up with a pocket full of cards with no idea where you met the people concerned or what you talked about. Transfer the information to your contacts book as soon as possible and have a small pocket address/contacts book in which to jot down information on people who don't give you cards.

Keep a full and accurate diary and write it up daily as well as using it for appointments. Winners not only know where they are going – they know where they have been and what happened because only in this way can they chart their wins and analyse the odd occasion on which they didn't win in order not to make the same mistake again.

… Practical winning

List making – a winning habit. Loads of lists means loads of wins – but for the moment think in terms of listing your jobs and goals for the day and tick off each one as it is completed. Enjoy the sense of accomplishment: you are winning with each job you tick off. While the idea of being a winner is a relatively new one, keep a list at home of the times you have proved to be a winner during the day and also the times you might have been more of a winner – and why. Don't brood – just make a note of how you could have done better. Very soon you'll find that winning is the rule and the rare times on which you don't win will be real surprises – in fact you'll even find yourself laughing about them.

At work keep lists recording wins by your team and department, both collective and individual. They can be a real morale booster especially at times when extra effort is indicated.

Live by the lists, not for the lists

Don't become obsessive! Lists, like plans, are there to help you become a winner so don't make more lists or plans than you can comfortably handle. Lists and plans are designed to save winners work because *work is something winners hate* and are determined to give up as far as is possible.

Decision time

Let us formalise these ideas to some extent by setting out a strategic pattern that encompasses much of what we have discussed so far.

Almost everyone wants to be a winner in every aspect of their lives but as none of us is exactly the same as any other person, even holistic winners may elect to devote more time and energy to winning in one department than another. The trick is to achieve the balance which will make you a winner while making the people with whom you come into contact winners as well.

Deciding on our strategic and tactical aims is difficult but the decisions are not immutable and, in fact, if we didn't change our minds at some stage it would mean that we had learned nothing – which would place us firmly among the losers. With this in mind, we can now put down on paper our long-term strategic aims, rating each aspect of our lives in accordance with its – current – importance. Remember – we are planning for perfection even if we do have to settle for a little less. Set down all your long-term winning aims, awarding points out of a hundred for importance. The categories might be, for example:

- wealth
- health
- attractive appearance
- power and influence
- a happy family life
- happy and successful children
- a respected place in the community
- fame

Ideally, perhaps we should have awarded ten importance points to each category, but in practice we have almost certainly split our list into two areas of importance and awarded more importance points to one area than the other so that we may, for instance, be over-emphasising Wealth, Power, Career Success, Fame and a Respected Place in the Community at the expense of the others or vice versa.

Holistic winning implies that winning in one area will help us achieve wins in other areas so, instead of awarding each category a number of importance points, let's regard each one as a building block with which we can build an extremely stable structure like a pyramid. This might yield something like:

Fame

Wealth, Power

Career Success, Successful Children, Respected Place

Health, Attractive Appearance, Happy Family Life, Happy Children

Now add in any extra strategic aims you may have thought of like Leisure or Cultural Development and build your own holistic winner's pyramid. You'll see that there are different ways of building your pyramid depending mainly on what you choose as the apex – but not so many as you might think.

You could try including some specifics in your building blocks, indicating that you want to be, for instance, a famous politician or a famous ballet dancer or that 'health' in your case depends to some extent on losing a couple of stone.

In most cases, deciding to become, say, a famous ballet dancer is meaningless without the lower steps of the pyramid. This doesn't mean that such a decision is fatuous in itself but merely that it should go into another category of 'overall' strategic decisions.

Plan Number One – the ultimate dream

Winners must have a dream because, although they may not be convinced that it really is better to 'travel hopefully' than to arrive, they know that in the long run it is hope that makes the journey bearable and can also make it fun.

Let's by all means dream about the super win that projects us into the International Household Name class, provided we remember that there is – or should be – only one heavyweight champion of the world and relatively few great painters, presidents or multi-millionaires.

Deciding from the beginning that we will derive no satisfaction from anything less than becoming the Champ, the Numero Uno or the wealthiest person in the world is the way to obsession. It may or may not make the realisation of any particular dream more likely but, by depriving us of the enjoyment of a myriad small and medium-sized wins along the way, it stands a very good chance of turning the dream into a nightmare.

Most of those who decide that only the ultimate goal is worthwhile must learn to live with the deadly poison of other people's success, while their own successes, however numerous, seem bitter and unsatisfying simply because they fall short of the ultimate triumph. Holistic winners do have an ultimate goal – or goals – but they are able to visualise their lives – past, present and future – as a whole, and they know there are opportunities for all of us to win hundreds of victories and that we should appreciate and celebrate them all.

Plan Number Two – the achievable dream

Perhaps your ultimate dream is to become an immortal literary figure and to take your place in the Pantheon alongside Shakespeare, Goethe, Dante and the rest. Why not? It's the sort of dream you can enjoy dreaming every now and again and it gives you a finite goal. Let's face it, though, not every writer is going to be read and quoted a thousand years from now and it would be a shame if the thought that you might not be among the few were to spoil your enjoyment of writing – or of your life.

Writing a best-seller, a prize-winning book or both, is probably the best achievable dream a writer can reasonably hope for and, rather like drawing a horse in the Irish Sweepstake, it brings with it a chance to win the ultimate prize, even though the odds may range from a million to one to odds on.

Plan Number Three – tactical dreaming

It's obvious – even though some people who dream of being writers don't seem to appreciate it – that the first and essential step in becoming the author of a best-selling book is to write a book and usually it helps to make it the best you are capable of writing. Then the book has to be brought to the attention of a publisher, who in turn has to submit it to the judgement of critics and the public. To reach the public, the writer must plan to submit the book himself, attempt to interest an agent, or have it printed privately and tour the country on horseback with book-filled saddle bags.

Plan Number Four – practical dreaming

Equally obvious – and equally incomprehensible to many people – is the fact that in order to write a book you have to put your bottom firmly on a seat in front of a computer and stay there with suitable breaks for wine, tea or whatever turns you on until several hundred pages of blank paper are covered with your golden words. As with most things, the best way to begin is to start. We can always change or even throw away what we have written.

Plan Number Five – pre-planning the dream

Most people have to earn a living while dreaming of immortality, in addition to which they usually have to gain some knowledge and/or experience before they begin. This is an important planning stage which could involve specialist education, a relevant associated occupation like journalism or a completely different specialist occupation which would yield memories or notebooks filled with usable plots, situations and characters.

Plan Number Six – the ultimate dream

A bit of a cheat this, since Plan Number One was the Ultimate Dream but let's go back to the Irish Sweepstake. Naturally you can't win without a ticket, but what makes you buy it? Usually the dream, however vague, that you might become the ultimate winner. Then you have to find the cash for a ticket, draw a horse and finally win the ultimate prize. The dream is no use without the ticket and the ticket is of little use without the dream.

Of course, the sort of planning we've been talking about doesn't apply merely to writing a book destined to become a classic. Much the same thing applies if our ultimate aim is to become a billionaire or a painter who will rank among the Masters.

In the winning scheme of things, the ultimate dream comes first – and last.

Tip from the Top

'No one plans to fail, but many fail to plan.'

'A plan is a dream with a deadline.'

8

Winners Don't Whine

What winners say is important, but often it's how they say it that makes all the difference. The way you speak can be one of the most important factors in making you a winner. Listen to someone you have already identified as a winner and ten to one he or she will be speaking clearly, distinctly and with interesting variations in pitch and tone.

Above all they will be speaking with quiet confidence. 'Quiet', because real winners do not have to bellow all the time although some of them have been known to shout when appropriate. Usually they find it quite sufficient to project their voices as actors do and you will usually find that in a social gathering, for example, although the winner may not be talking more loudly than the other people – often in fact quite the opposite – it will be the winner's voice that you hear clearly among all the conversational 'rhubarb'.

Some years ago there was an advertisement that appeared in a great many papers and magazines which ran 'Are you strangled by the Old School Tie when the power to speak could free you?' The implication was that if you had not been to a public school, you were disadvantaged and learning how to speak correctly could redress the balance. In those days 'correctly' meant with a standard English or public school accent and a couple of decades or so ago it was absolutely true that anyone who didn't speak standard English was handicapped while anyone who spoke the public school version of standard English was privileged. Of course, no one can say that, in England at any rate, this form of snobbery no longer exists. It does, and in certain circumstances, it is no bad thing to be able to speak standard English. However, thanks largely to radio and TV, regional accents have become acceptable and some, in fact, very acceptable indeed. Scottish has always been more acceptable than most other accents but now Welsh and Irish are perfectly okay in Britain and in some places in the world a great deal more acceptable than an English accent.

Nowadays a regional accent is no bar to becoming a winner. Besides, it is easy enough to become bilingual if you wish and winners are often linguistic chameleons who adapt their accent to the company and the circumstances. Everyone does this to some extent by modifying their accent and the way they speak – not to mention what they say – when they are out with friends as compared with, say, at home or in the workplace. Winners merely develop this ability which is often a question of shading, rather than changing one's accent completely. You don't have to speak perfect Scouse, for example, to be accepted in a Liverpool pub, but if you have a Public School accent you might find it politic to modify it slightly. Winners are socially mobile.

Accentuate the accent

The main thing winners have to learn is not to be worried or ashamed about whatever accent they may have. If you are worried about the way you speak, change it. If you find you are unable to change it, make a feature of it so that it becomes a part of your personality, as a number of top TV personalities, not to mention film stars, do these days.

You could decide to retain your accent as your trademark but – and this is a big 'but' – if you decide to retain your accent, this is no excuse for speaking badly. Winners' voices are never monotonous, whatever their accent: in fact a monotonous whine tags you as a loser.

Incidentally, if you have a speech impediment, this is no longer the drawback it once was and you can take comfort from the large number of radio and TV personalities who began life with similar handicaps.

Can that be me?

Ask someone with a tape recorder to record some of your ordinary conversation, if possible when you are not aware they are doing so, and then play it back. Your first reaction could well be that of many broadcasters on hearing themselves for the first time, namely 'That can't be me.' It is!

Now you know what you sound like and, if you are unhappy with what you hear, you can use the tape recorder to help you modify the way you speak. You will almost certainly, for instance, wish to speak more clearly because winners can't win unless they get their winning message across.

Male winners may wish to pitch their voices a little deeper than they are when they first hear themselves on tape. This is only a question of practice. In the same way, many women may find they wish to speak a little more softly. Using the voice correctly is an essential weapon in the winner's armoury in most circumstances, but it is also an acceptable way of using sex in social and working situations.

Think of a few ways in which you have used your voice recently to help you get what you want – in other words to be a winner – or times when having a more attractive voice might have been useful. Winners find that attractive speaking voices help make them winners all through the day for every day of their lives and they don't even have to think about it. So, if your voice needs changing, use the tape recorder to help you change it.

Learning to read

Oh really! This is too much. I wouldn't have bought the book if I hadn't been able to read. Quite right – you can read; most of us can, but can you get words off a page? Try reading a few paragraphs from a newspaper, a poem or a play script, which you can borrow from your local library, into a tape recorder – you can practise first if you like. Then play it back and you will realise why even some professional actors occasionally find it difficult to 'get words off the page'.

Reading aloud is an art and a particularly useful one for winners so even if it sounds stiff and unnatural at first, do persevere. If you find it embarrassing even though you are by yourself, try using comic voices to make yourself laugh before going on. Later you may wish to use your partner as a sounding board to check your progress and to comment. Whatever you do, keep the first tapes you make. They could give you a giggle – and a genuine sense of achievement – when you play them back in a week or so's time. Don't forget, if you already have a 'good' accent and perfect speaking voice as well as superb delivery you may wish to use the recorder to help with your ability to modify these factors when appropriate.

Winning roles

Try playing out imaginary scenes featuring your colleagues and bosses in different situations. Imagine, for instance, that you are in the boss's office discussing your request for something fairly minor – say a car space or a new drinks machine for the office. Try it once with the boss in a good mood and once with the boss in a foul temper.

Remember you are concentrating on getting your voice right but, at the same time, bear in mind that winners are expert at what may be called verbal judo. The art of judo involves using the strength of the other person's attack against him and verbal judo works in much the same way.

Winners do not say, 'You are absolutely wrong' – they do say, 'You could be right but I've given it a lot of thought and …' or 'What you say is very interesting but …' Try to convey this attitude by your tone of voice rather than words, using the tape recorder to check the impression you hope to make.

Man's best friend – the dog and bone

When it comes to winning, one of man's best friends – and woman's too – is the telephone and it can help you be a winner both in the workplace and in the social sphere.

Winners tend to use the phone a great deal, not only because it is quick and convenient, but because it is a first class way of bringing their winning personalities to bear. Also, while they don't use the phone to deceive people in any unpleasant way, winners are fully aware of the fact that the phone enables them to present themselves in the best possible light at times when a personal confrontation might be less flattering. Winners, for example, seldom get hangovers, but you could imagine an occasion on which you feel really rough because of a cold or a hangover and practice projecting on the phone the impression of a fit, confident individual, bright-eyed, bushy-tailed – and definitely a winner.

Most of the time, however, the winner will use the phone in a more straightforward way to achieve whatever it is he or she wishes. To do this, make use of a curious fact of electronics which you have probably noticed in your experiments with the tape recorder, namely that electronic equipment accentuates vocal characteristics, accents and above all emotions. This is particularly true of the telephone which can pick up fear or indecision quicker than a lie detector and at the same time is capable of accentuating a speaker's feeling of happiness or confidence. A telephone can even pick up a smile, which is why winners spend a lot of time smiling into the phone. So much so that a winner using the phone when in good form could easily be mistaken for something of a headcase. This is because the winner is acting into the phone – smiling, shaking her head, gesticulating, frowning and so on as though the person at the other end of the line were sitting at the other side of the desk. This is the winning way to use the phone and once you have mastered it, you will never look back.

... Practical winning

Using the tape recorder and an unplugged phone, try using the acting-into-the-phone technique to persuade a colleague to change her day off, to ask your boss a favour you know he won't be too happy to grant or to tell your best beloved you won't be able to get home for your anniversary.

Don't forget to phone

As we have stressed, winners use the phone a lot and this is partly because phones build up brownie points at work and on the home front. This doesn't mean that you have to be on the phone either to your boss or your loved one every five minutes, but people do like to be kept informed. You can be the best salesperson in the world for instance, but if you are in the field and lose contact with the office for days at a time, you are going to give your boss ulcers, which is not a winning move. At the same time, your wife or husband is going to forgive almost anything provided he or she knows that you have not run off with a new lover – or been flattened by a bus.

Technology now gives you an amazing new raft of gadgets and techniques for keeping in touch, with emails, WAP phones, texting and personal digital assistants (PDAs). There is a tendency amongst the younger and more with-it generation to flog these technologies to the nth degree, but winners need to beware the pitfalls of lapsing into digi-speak or emoticons. These do not smack of winning and are often used to impress mates rather than to properly augment a winning image.

Of course, these technologies are very useful in their immediacy and their ability to bridge space and national boundaries, and they can greatly aid organisational progress and communication. Such facilities as teleconferencing, for instance, can link winners from across the globe in a way that was impossible a decade ago. Use these technologies wisely, remembering always that you *are* a winner and that nothing should detract from that fact. For more information, see *How To Change Your Life with Technology*, by Anthony Capstick, Management Books 2000.

Finally – the first word

A lot of people, who on all other occasions use the phone like winners by really projecting their personalities, answer the phone with a colourless 'hello' as though they were about to expire at any moment. Winners know that the 'Hello!' sets the tone of the whole conversation that follows and is in fact the all-important first contact. Answer the phone with a cheerful 'Hello!' or even 'Good Morning, Fred Bloggs ...' and use the recorder to test the impression you make – it should be one that will help to make you a winner.

Tip from the Top

'Communicate to accumulate.'

9

Fit To Win

Being a winner means being in control of ourselves, of events and of other people. As we have seen, we can begin to get the winning habit by taking control of our own lives in such seemingly trivial areas as deciding the time at which we get up in the morning. What we have done by getting up earlier is to begin winning by making decisions in an area in which we might be expected to have maximum control.

We can now look for similar areas, one of which is our own body. Unless we are extremely ill, our body is one thing about which we and we alone take decisions so it is an area in which we can win; so much so that even some prisoners, who have lost control over virtually every other aspect of their lives, take an interest in building up their physique as being one of the areas in which they can still win.

You too can have a body

You don't have to be a top class athlete to be a winner, but athletes do tend to be winners in other spheres than their own sport, largely because they are fit, poised and confident. In other words, they look and behave like winners. Fortunately, most of us can attain fitness, poise and confidence without winning Olympic medals and, once we are reasonably fit, a few minutes a day is usually all the time it takes to maintain that air of physical well-being and mental alertness that says 'winner'.

The bad news is that you may not be as 'reasonably' fit as you think you are because, unless you fall ill, being unfit creeps up on you without your realising it. The good news is that you can usually become much fitter without giving up all the good things in life.

One way of finding out exactly how fit you are is to have a full scale medical check-up, but that can be fairly expensive. Alternatively, you could ask your own doctor to run the rule over you to make sure that there is nothing radically and obviously wrong and then do a test at a reputable fitness centre. Naturally, these people are after your business but they will give you a test, usually for a small set fee, and let you know how fit you are and how you could improve. You could even find that it is worthwhile joining a fitness centre, but try to get a week or so on a trial basis before committing yourself to a full year.

Knowing how you are just now will give you a sound basis on which to take actions to rectify any actual problems, correct imbalances and install precautionary measures against potential problems, for a good future.

Health and the take PAINS and ACT formula

If we check the advantages of a thorough health check against our 'Winning When the Sky Falls In' formula, we can see that this one move alone can help counter a great many potential and actual disasters:

- **Posture** – Depending on the results of the check, people either know that they are reasonably fit – which is a great confidence booster – or, if something amiss has been revealed, they know exactly what it is and have an idea how to deal with it.
- **Avoidance** – The check-up provides an opportunity to reverse harmful trends and thus avoid many health hazards altogether.
- **Insurance** – Here the insurance is against the possibility of a serious illness remaining undiagnosed. Financial insurance against the effects of illness and injury are another matter, but one result of having a check-up is often to make people think in terms of this type of insurance.
- **Assessment** – Disasters revealed by thorough medical examinations of this sort fall into two main categories: previously undiagnosed illnesses and the cumulative effects of unhealthy living. In both cases, while it may be unpleasant to hear that all is not well, the advantages of early diagnosis are obvious.
- **Counter-measures** – In the case of an illness being diagnosed the clinic will often recommend specialist treatment, but in the case of patients whose life-style is making future health trouble almost inevitable, while some clinics provide help in the form of, say, diet sheets or useful addresses, they usually confine themselves to giving advice.
- Termination of cause of disaster – In cases where an unhealthy life-style is seen as a potential cause of disaster, it's up to those of us who wish to win to consider carefully any professional advice we are given. This is often a question of finding a diet and a method of exercising that suits us and for winners this means food and exercise we can enjoy.

Go for the glow

When it comes to physical exercise, winners don't 'go for the burn' – instead they go for the 'glow' that comes from exercising without strain and well within their capabilities. The secret is that, like all winning, it has to be fun and the fun lies in feeling one's capabilities extend from day to day.

Aim to achieve the ebullient sparkle that goes with glowing health by combining a diet of tasty and interesting food and drink with a course of exercise which is sufficiently varied not to be boring. Boredom is the enemy of the winner and boredom is the curse of many diets and exercise programmes.

The great thing about aiming for the sort of fitness we describe is that you can actually feel – and see – yourself winning. Achieving the sort of fitness we are talking about does involve dieting if you are overweight but, in much the same way as we advise winners to work less rather than more, we advise people who want to lose weight to eat and drink better things rather than starve themselves.

Living on lettuce leaves and water is a concept totally abhorrent to winners, so we advise eating and drinking the best of everything.

A winning workout should be something you enjoy so if, for instance, you like swimming, make a regular visit to the baths a major part of your workout programme. If, on the other hand, you hate swimming, but still appreciate that it is superb all round exercise, restrict it to a minor role in your workout programme. Some exercise is boring beyond belief but, using the Judo technique which we have already mentioned as part of the winner's armoury, it is possible to turn even this to advantage.

For example, if you are using an exercise bike – which is about as much fun as watching paint dry – you can use a cassette player to learn a foreign language. We know someone who picked up a university degree largely as a result of listening to tapes and reading while using an exercise bike and a rowing machine. This is a winning move in two ways because you are becoming an expert at something and therefore a winner, while the fact that you are not thinking about your exercising means that you will exercise more naturally and almost certainly for a longer time.

Winners invariably do two or more things at once

Winners can't help doing more than one thing at once, mainly because almost every winning move they make has a knock-on effect, so that, for example, becoming fitter doesn't affect only health – although this in itself is of vital importance. At the same time as we become fitter, we gain in confidence, we change the way in which people look at us and, as our clothes hang better, we begin to look better dressed. We should also find that mentally we are a great deal more alert than when we were unfit. This is yet another example of the snowball factor.

It's obvious that even the lowliest member of an organisation can become a winner in this way by becoming a person glowing with health and vitality. Mind you, glowing is usually quite sufficient and it is not a winning move to do triple somersaults into your boss's office if he happens to be a sixty-five-year-old, twenty-stone, arthritis sufferer.

Winners do not show off. Of course, this doesn't mean that they pass up on opportunities to demonstrate their excellence or expertise, merely that they pick their moments.

Fitness is a typical example of the cumulative effect of winning and acquiring winning habits which we have variously referred to as the 'snowball effect' or the 'knock-on effect', in order to stress the fact that wins, however small, rarely occur in a vacuum, and that a win in one sphere will almost certainly lead to wins in others.

We can see this very clearly in the case of the spin-off wins we get as a bonus once we achieve the ideal level of fitness. We've noticed that we feel more alert and have a better posture and walk, all of which give us an immediate bonus in the workplace because it is something that other people, especially bosses, tend to notice. Another bonus is that our clothes feel better and look better – as well as, curiously enough, more expensive. Because of this, people tend to look on us more as winners than they may have done before, which encourages us to pursue a winning path.

Winners excel – at some things

Winners like to win things although they are not obsessively competitive. In other words, they like to win relatively easily and certainly without killing themselves in the process. 'Effortless' is the word that comes to mind when one thinks of sports people, for example, who are genuine winners.

Taking up a sport can help enormously. Of course, being a winner at abseiling or canoeing won't guarantee promotion in the workplace but these things do make you feel like a winner and they can also help develop latent powers of leadership – so much so that many large firms are now paying for their executives to take part in sports and more particularly in the Outward Bound type of activity which has a more immediate and obvious application in promoting leadership qualities useful in the workplace.

Being fit is fine, but don't worry if you are not the athletic type. A win is a win is a win and if you can become a champion at tiddlywinks or mumbledy peg you will still experience the 'rush' that comes from winning and go on to win more.

A win is a win is a win

The important thing in being a winner is to win and, outside the office or the workshop, there is a whole world in which to win and multifarious ways in which to become a winner. Imagine, for instance, that you were to take up an exotic and gentle form of unarmed combat and become a Brown or even a Black Belt. Come to think of it, even a Yellow Belt – which means you are considered just about teachable – is enough to make you walk tall. Make a list of sports, hobbies and other activities you might wish to pursue, especially those about which you have always said 'I'd like to try my hand at that.'

A win is a win – is a parachute

You might even think about winning at a hobby, for example, which could make you a little money – so that, almost without thinking, you will not only have chalked up a win but at the same time prepared yourself the beginnings of a parachute. As we said earlier, winners always try to accomplish at least two things at once.

Taking control of your body and your appearance is an ideal example of how to be a winner as the victories are many, and usually quantifiable. In fact, for the first few weeks or so – perhaps even longer – it should be possible to mark up *at least one win a day*.

A book of victories

It's worthwhile keeping a special diary, in addition to the complete record of your journey on the road to becoming a winner, in which to note down your victories on the way to fitness. Write down on the first page your measurements, weight and so on, and whether you want to increase or decrease your weight. If you take a fitness test before starting, make sure you get a copy of the results and enter them in your diary. You should also enter your performance details, for example, '3 minutes on exercise bike at low resistance, five sit ups, jogged 200 yards', and so on.

Unless you are already very fit you can almost guarantee that, looking back at your diary after a couple of weeks, your performance on the first day will seem pathetic but, for the moment, aim each day for an increase in the numbers of at least one of the exercises you do and don't forget that every improvement is a win. In many ways, the more unfit you are at the moment the more obvious will be the improvement. But don't forget – take it easy and go for the glow.

... Practical winning

Jot down the names of any actors or actresses you regard as winners, especially if you have a photograph of them to hand. They may not necessarily be perfect physical types but most of them will glow with health and exude the sort of confidence that physical well-being confers.

Do the same thing with people you know well, especially those with whom you come into contact at work. Whatever their physical type, most of the people you select as winners will look alert, confident and, though far from bumptious, will certainly not be lacking in self-esteem.

Next, try to conjure up the names of a few people you think of as losers and see how they match up with the fit-looking winners.

Which set of people do you think would be better able to handle disaster?

Now look into the mirror and try to see yourself through the eyes of a stranger. Write down your observations in detail and, if you are brave enough, ask a couple of friends for their comments.

Tip from the Top

'Winning is constantly improving everything.'

10

Winners Deserve the Best

Winners deserve their rewards: every victory, however small, should be rewarded. As a winner, if you have people working for you, you will know how much rewards are appreciated, even if they are nothing more than a smile or a verbal pat on the back.

Your own managers, however, may not be quite so perceptive and, although in the long run you should be able to educate them by example, in the meantime, when you chalk up a victory, you should celebrate by rewarding yourself. Even the smallest win is worth a small smile of self-congratulations and, while smirking is definitely a no-no, there is no earthly reason why you should not look cheerful if you have just proved yourself a winner.

If only our old teachers had concentrated on making us pleased with ourselves, and even allowing us to show it, instead of accentuating the mediocre and preaching the joys of conformity! Years later, in the forces and at work, clones of these depressing tyrants are still shouting 'You're not here to think!' or 'You're not here to enjoy yourselves!' to which even an apprentice winner replies – though perhaps sotto voce – 'Of course we bloody are!'

The great thing about being a winner is that you are pleased with yourself in the sense of the French phrase we use meaning 'happy in one's skin'. This, of course, has nothing to do with self-satisfaction which upsets people and is therefore counter-productive, but means simply that winners are pleased to be who they are, pleased to be doing what they are doing, happy to be winning and not particularly anxious to change places with anyone on earth.

Winners deserve the best

A quiet smile is a fine reward for those tiny victories winners experience all the time, but the win of the day, the win of the week or the *win of the month* deserves something a little more extravagant. Reward yourself for these with something positive and combine the rewards you give yourself with your winner's appreciation of excellence so that, in effect, you are – yet again – winning twice.

It needn't cost the earth. In fact, a win of the day could be celebrated at the cost of a few pence by changing your evening drink from, say, a pint of beer to a glass of malt whisky or fine wine.

Fine feathers

Among those material possessions that tell others something about the sort of people winners are, clothes rank very highly, so it makes sense to reward ourselves for a reasonably important win by buying an item of clothing – it should be the best you can afford of its kind.

Be extravagant in small things. It's useful to remember that the ideal present is something, however small, which is so extravagant that you wouldn't normally dream of buying it for yourself. In the case of a winner buying a reward, this is exactly what you do buy yourself. Not only does the reward make you feel good, and therefore more of a winner, but the raw silk tie or the hand-made shoes will lift whatever else you happen to be wearing into the winning bracket.

If it's something to wear, or to carry with you, your reward could become a trademark. A bow tie, for instance, has been used by several winning personalities to help them stand out from the crowd by giving them instant recognition. The same effect can be achieved by, say, an unusual watch, earrings or cuff-links.

Another useful reward item which could become a trademark is a really good fountain pen, especially if you work in an office where pens are always in use and always in evidence. So use, for instance, a pen with a broad, bold nib for signing your letters and practise a powerful 'winning' signature, especially if sending out letters under your name is part of your job. For meetings, interviews and such like, a silver or stainless-steel ball-point is okay. Never use a bog-standard plastic biro at work – it is not a winner's sign.

Be generous with stationery, whether you are writing letters for your organisation or for yourself. This doesn't mean you have to make paper aeroplanes out of the stuff, but it does mean allowing generous margins and spacing and a signature big enough to show you mean business. Letter writing is an important way of selling yourself as a winner and one which costs nothing but a little thought. Try to send out all letters, especially business letters, without mistakes, but whatever you do, don't send scrunched up, mean looking letters with apologetic signatures. Try to avoid sending out hand-written envelopes.

Make an exhibition of yourself

Another piece of schoolday advice winners can do without is 'Don't make an exhibition of yourself' because, unless you can afford to pay a high priced PR man to do the job for you, you have to make an exhibition of yourself if you are going to be a winner.

Of course, there is a lot of difference between making an exhibition of oneself in the sense we mean and behaving like a total idiot. But while a great deal depends on the individual's personality, the only place where you are likely to win by appearing to be a total non-entity is aboard a hijacked aircraft. In most other cases, getting yourself favourably noticed is a winning move. You have to sell yourself to be a winner and you should be your own best Public Relations Consultant.

... Practical winning

Imagine that you are a top executive of a multinational PR company, who has just been given you as a client. The aim is to get your client noticed and to present him as a winner. You should try a couple of proposals, one for a limited budget and one where you can spend a little more money. Try to think up one or more down-to-earth schemes but, at the same time, try to come up with something really off-beat. Let your subconscious work for you on this one. You could easily come up with a winner.

We know one chap, for instance, who went out one day and bought himself an elderly Lagonda, in the days when such things were merely expensive rather than prohibitive, and found he had acquired an instant 'trademark' which was a genuine winner.

Share your wins – and your rewards

There's a lot of truth in the old saying about a trouble shared being a trouble halved. We all need a shoulder to cry on at times and most of us who have partners use them as sounding boards when we want to have a good moan. That's fine as long as it's not overdone and as long as there's a two-way traffic in damp shoulders. For winners, it is much more important to remember that *a win shared is a win doubled.*

When the homecomer answers the time-honoured question, 'What sort of a day did you have?' with 'Pretty good actually. In fact I picked up a bottle of decent plonk to celebrate. If you like I'll tell you about it while we have a glass or two,' the win is shared, celebrated and reinforced all at the same time. It also makes for a much better atmosphere than a non-committal growl and, as allowing someone into a part of your life they don't always share completely is something of an intimacy reinforcer, this makes for yet another win.

Share your wins in the workplace too, especially if colleagues have contributed towards the victory. It needn't be anything big – a box of chocolates or a bottle of wine, for example, is hardly going to break you as a way of saying 'thank you' to the team that helped you achieve great sales figures or whatever, but it counts a hell of a lot more than the thought and in some cases more than money.

When you are rewarding yourself though for a really big win, think of something you have always wanted and, if you can reasonably (or even unreasonably) afford it, treat yourself. It could be anything from a new hairdo to a world cruise, with lots of scope in between, from a new car to a visit to a health farm.

Make a list of the rewards you would like to give yourself for wins, ranging from the smallest to the biggest you can think of. Remember that winners, while they do try to put something by for a rainy day, are rarely miserly or anxious to make a good showing in the 'Recent Wills' column of their local paper.

... Practical winning

Maybe your list of treats looks like this – Holiday; Weekend at Health Farm; New Car; New Clothes; Watch; Jewellery; Furniture.

There's a nasty puritanical streak about those people who are convinced that there is something fundamentally wrong about enjoying the rewards of winning, whatever they may be, and that spending the money you have earned on the good things of life is especially wicked.

We firmly believe that this is total rubbish and that, once you have taken care of things like food and housing for yourself and your dependents, and perhaps sent a few bob to those who have little chance to win, you should concentrate on the things you enjoy.

Whatever your favourite cliché relating to the taboo subject of death, it really is true that 'we pass this way but once' and 'in the midst of life ...' etc. Winners are here to enjoy themselves in the workplace, in the home, the pub, the theatre, the country – wherever.

Tip from the top

'Little things do mean a lot.'

11

Winning Teams

Once you know what to look for it's pretty easy to spot winners as people who are poised, confident, fit-looking and above all, happy, as we put it, 'in their skin'. In fact, they might just as well be wearing badges proclaiming their winning status, but what is particularly striking is that almost all of them seem to be members of a winning team.

There are some winners who are loners but, if so, it is always from choice and if they are, for example, freelancers in the workplace they will usually be found to be working for winning clients, perhaps in addition to being members of a winning team on the leisure front. For the most part, winners are to be found in winning teams and it should not come as a shock for us to learn that this is not a coincidence.

Of course, winners do create winning teams and this is a very important part of being a winner. But often, especially in the workplace, a much easier way is to join a winning team.

Finding a winning team

Before you can join a winning team you have to find one. Curiously enough, identifying a winning team is as easy to do, and as difficult to define, as identifying and defining an individual winner. Winning groups do share many of the characteristics of the winning individuals we have been looking at. Naturally, not all the winning teams we are considering wear identifying jerseys. At first sight, some of them may not even look like teams at all because the winning teams we mean range from small offices to multi-national industries and from infantry sections to vast armies.

However, since the principles involved are much the same for all groups it will be helpful to look first at teams that do wear jerseys and you could begin by making a list of some of the sporting teams past and present that have been genuine winners. You could then list some of their characteristics; for example:

(1) Winning teams have a great many winners in them; most of the players are poised, confident, etc. and although they may well be 'stars' in their own right they are confident enough to allow others to shine and to help them to be winners.

(2) Winning teams have the winning habit and because they usually have more winning games behind them than otherwise they go into every game expecting to win.

(3) Winning teams often include winning groups and combinations, like a winning forward line or a winning defence, which work together so well they sometimes seem to have a sixth sense, whereas in fact they have merely learned to co-operate to make each other winners and to make the team a winning team.

(4) Winning teams develop a special energy that comes from winning and which increases not by simple progression but geometrically, which means that a group of, say, four winners doesn't have the winning energy of four individual winners but a great deal more. (This is called synergy.)

(5) A winning team develops both mental and physical energy. It can withstand adversity better than a losing team, coming back for more when defeat seems almost inevitable – not to mention doing a strenuous lap of honour when victory is finally achieved.

(6) Winning teams create a winning atmosphere. Their winning aura may even surround the 'losing' team so that all the spectators go away happy – as winners – and the losing team shares in the glamour of 'a match to remember', having raised their game to the best of which they are capable. Everyone, in fact, emerges a winner.

(7) With a winning team, winning is contagious so that newcomers soon acquire the team's magic – but they do have to be playing in the right league.

Of course, all sorts of forces tend to ensure that football players, soldiers, executives and the rest of us do not play out of our leagues and it should happen less often to a winner than others.

However, should you find yourself playing in the wrong league – for whatever reason – move!!

This applies particularly in the workplace where sociologists have identified the Peter Principle, or a tendency to promote people to positions just beyond their capabilities, which is a total *no-win* situation, both for the individual and the team concerned. The first remedy is to move to another department or even another organisation and then perhaps to consider the possibilities like retraining, additional experience and so on.

Remember ... a winner can win in any league – except the wrong one.

Joining a winning team – in the workplace

As we have seen, there are winning teams in every league and, as even winners have to begin somewhere, it is as well, especially in the working context, to join a winning team. Later, for the experienced winner, for whom winning has become a habit, there will be advantages – and a great deal of satisfaction – to be gained by joining a team which has winning potential and turning it round. But for the moment let's think about joining a ready-made winning team. To do this, we need to know what sort of organisation we intend joining. Even when jobs are hard to come by, it is worthwhile making a few inquiries about the state of industrial relations in our proposed workplace.

Aggro is for losers and winners aren't doormats – precisely the opposite – but they don't go looking for a fight, so it's well worthwhile having a chat with someone who already works in your intended workplace, preferably in a similar job to the one you are after or even in the same department. Very often newspapers and libraries can be useful sources of information as to whether or not the organisation you intend joining is a winner.

A history of industrial disputes, for example, especially over trivial matters, might make you think twice, while glowing tributes at retirement parties combined with lots of success stories would be encouraging.

For the genuine winner in the workplace, winning is not a question of putting one over on either colleagues or management. In the same way, in a winning organisation, whether it is a tiny office or a multinational concern, winning, for management, is not a question of conning the individual into doing more work for less. In fact, a winning organisation – like a winning individual – will attempt to do away with as much 'work' as possible by making employment enjoyable.

When we look at the sort of things which persuade us to undertake any particular form of activity, we are talking about motivation and when the activity is in the workplace we are talking about industrial motivation. So – especially in the workplace – what are the sort of things that are liable to get us, and the people who work with us, for us, or under us, up off our butts.

What makes Johnny run? It's not just money – by a long chalk

Make no mistake, most winners like money and the things money can buy as much as anyone, but motivation experts identify no less than sixteen non-financial motivating factors. These include:

(1) Fear

In the bad old days, fear was often the physical fear of being hurt. There were any number of physical punishments, from flogging to torture and even execution. Fortunately, in modern times, the physical fear does not apply. Instead, we have many mental fears of which, curiously enough, one of the main ones is the fear of doing the wrong thing. There is also the fear of making fools of ourselves and the fear of getting caught if we know we have done wrong. Fear is more a manipulative factor than a motivating factor, but it is so important that it must head any list of motivations. History has many examples of leaders using fear as their main weapon. One fear that many people have is the fear of losing their job, and the fear of being poor.

→ **Winners are less fearful than most people.**

(2) Greed

We wouldn't be human if we didn't sometimes want a little bit more. Usually, we are too embarrassed to display greed publicly, but in ourselves we usually want that little bit extra – the biggest piece of cake, a larger house, and of course more money.

→ **Winners are only human in this respect but they don't allow greed to rule their lives.**

(3) Competition

Most people are highly competitive. A small number of people are so competitive that they always want to be top or the best. The majority of people, however, are in a smaller category and, while they are not prepared to go to extremes to be absolutely at the top, nevertheless do not want to be beaten by their peers or anyone they consider inferior. Competition not to be bottom of the league is often more powerful than competition to reach the top. Realistically, many people are content to be in the middle, but if their rankings start to drop they will immediately become more competitive.

→ **Winners enjoy competitions they can win. They can be serious, but rarely deadly serious, about competition and tend to appreciate its 'game play' aspect.**

(4) Recognition

This is a posh word for saying 'thank you'. 'It costs nothing to be polite.' Saying 'thank you' is good manners and is always appreciated. Adults, just like children and animals, like to be thanked frequently. There is a tendency to believe that saying 'thank you' is demeaning, but this is simply not true. It makes both the giver and the receiver feel good.

→ **Manners maketh winners.**

(5) Pride

Be proud of what you do and who you do it for. It is no good being apologetic and ashamed of your occupation. Every single person in every organisation, however large, is important. However lowly you may think you are, you are nevertheless playing a vital role. We do not know of anyone who is intentionally paid for doing nothing. Military people of all nations are experts in the use of pride as a motivation factor; so much so that they can sometimes persuade people to die for it.

→ **Winners walk tall and, as they used to say in the army, with 'bags of swank'.**

(6) Involvement

Getting involved is very motivating, but sometimes people don't know how to start. The best way to get involved, and to show that you want to get involved, is to ask questions. Asking questions shows that you are taking an interest as well as getting involved. Another way of getting involved is to constantly look at ways of improving what you are doing and the environment in which you work. Very small ideas for change are a form of involvement. Be prepared to challenge statements like 'We've always done it that way.' Involvement is one of the key areas in which you can enjoy your work more and it is easy to get started.

→ **Winners ask questions to learn – and question assumptions to live.**

(7) Belonging

It is very motivating to feel part of a winning team, club, village, or any identifiable group. British people are very keen on joining clubs and the feeling of belonging is very strong. The opposite to belonging is being 'left out', which is not always very comfortable.

→ **Winners enjoy belonging and, as they tend to be good company, are usually sought after.**

(8) Status

British people are still very class conscious, which means they are status conscious too. Again, military people are great experts in status, only they call it by a different name, rank. They are also very clever to give each rank a different uniform or badge. Status in civilian life is much more subtle, but nevertheless is extremely important. Job titles in effect define a form of status and therefore should be as descriptive and as positive as possible. Status symbols are a clever commercial exploitation of this motivation factor.

→ **Winners usually enjoy status, and even status symbols, as much as anyone but they don't need them in order to be identified as winners.**

(9) Fun

Smiling and enjoying ourselves is actually healthy! Why shouldn't we enjoy our lives more? In fact, the whole of this book is intended to emphasise this point. Make it a habit to smile more and you will find it is infectious and people invariably smile back. It is just as easy to develop the habit to smile as it is to scowl, so be positive and enjoy yourself.

→ **Winners enjoy life.**

(10) Challenge

Big challenges can be intimidating, but small challenges can be motivating. The small challenges often begin with the phrase 'Bet you can't!' Bet you can't finish this by Friday is a challenge that many people can't resist. It also stirs the competitive spirit. However, if the challenge is too great then it will not be taken up and this will be demotivating. Look for the small challenges and each challenge achieved is a minor win. At a more advanced level, events like the London Marathon offer a tremendous challenge, not only to the 'elite' athletes who start at the front and can reckon to finish in world-class times, but to the ordinary Joe and Jane who do it as a personal challenge and to help raise cash for others.

→ **Winners begin by challenging themselves.**

(11) Adventure

A new experience is an adventure. All change can be treated as an adventure. We look for adventure as part of our holidays so why shouldn't we look for adventure at work. By calling a new task an adventure you can catch people's imagination and get their co-operation as well.

→ **For the winner, all life is an adventure, whether it involves the body or the mind.**

(12) Helping others

Helping others less fortunate than ourselves can be very motivating. Contributing to charity is an obvious way to help others, and it is amazing how motivating some fund-raising is. Sponsored swims, sponsored walks, sponsored runs are an everyday occurrence and are enjoyed by many.

→ **Winners are no slouches when it comes to charity and good works but have also been known to help people more fortunate than themselves.**

The final four

Leadership

The word 'leader' is an intimidating one and builds the picture of a great leader like Churchill or Napoleon. In fact, most of the world is run by 'little' leaders and one definition of a leader is simply 'the person in charge'. In business, the leader is called a manager, a supervisor, a chargehand, etc. etc. Every team or group of people must have somebody in charge and that person is the leader. The most effective team size is ten or eleven people or even smaller. The Roman army, for example, had sections of ten, and most sports have teams of eleven, of whom one is a playing leader or captain.

A number of writers on leadership would argue that a true leader only leads with the acceptance of the led, that managing and leading are different and that anyone could be a manager, but only people with the added ingredient of personal engagement with the led can be leaders.

In the workplace, the leader usually has managerial duties in addition to other duties, but this is not essential. The leader may, in fact, be doing an identical job to his team mates as in many sports. However, it is essential that every member of the team knows who the leader is as the lack of a clear system and purpose is very demotivating and leads to chaos.

→ **Winners are often those people others look to for leadership, especially in times of crisis.**

Planning

Every team has a plan and the leader is in charge of the plan. No one plans to fail, but many fail to plan. There must be a plan whether it is a five-year plan, a one-year plan, a one-month plan, a one-week plan, a one-day plan, a one-morning, a one-hour plan or a one-minute plan. Without proper planning, nothing will work effectively. Ideally, plans should be written down and shared wherever possible. Ownership of the plan by the team is one of the essential ingredients for winning.

→ **Winners plan to win.**

Deadlines

If you have forever to do something, that is exactly how long it will take. All plans must have a deadline, and this deadline should be practical and visible. Deadlines are very motivating as everybody hates to miss a deadline. Missing a deadline is losing, and beating a deadline is winning.

→ **Winners arrange to meet their deadlines – without actually panting.**

Achievement

Achievement is the satisfaction of finishing the job. On time! It can be the satisfaction of crossing off the task from your list. It is the most motivating of all the factors because it can be summed up in one word. Winning!

Tip from the Top

'Show me a good loser and I'll show you a loser.'

12

Winners like to say 'yes'

Winners like to say 'yes' because it makes the other person feel like a winner and helps spread the winning feeling throughout the home or the workplace. They know that saying 'yes' to another person's request can be a subtle form of 'stroking' because, whether they are being asked for the loan of a pencil or a hefty rise, the decision-making process is an exercise of power.

Because they are aware of this – either consciously or subconsciously – winners prefer to say 'yes' graciously, or at least not grudgingly. Their decision in some cases may be the same as that of the non-winner but whereas the non-winner will make it obvious that a favour is being granted reluctantly, the winner will make it plain that the favour, once decided on, has been granted willingly.

Of course, there are times when even winners can't be expected to make on-the-spot decisions. But these won't usually be questions of whether or not to lend a pencil or any other relatively trivial matter and even in such cases the winner will normally explain why a decision can't be made at once and, more importantly, say exactly when a decision can be expected.

In most day-to-day exchanges, however, the winner will have the confidence to make an immediate decision and will not only do his or her best to say 'yes' but will use the opportunity to make the other person feel even more of a winner by using words like 'certainly', 'glad to be of help' or 'let's give it a go.'

Difficult decisions

Naturally, in the real world, not all requests can be granted immediately, or even granted at all, but there is a tremendous difference between a 'That's a tough one but we'll see what we can do' and a non-negotiable 'Can't be done.'

Winners are quite capable of pointing out how difficult it may be to fulfil any given request, but they won't make it out to be more difficult than it is, and if things are going to take some time they will normally explain why this is the case. They will also try, wherever possible, to give the explanations themselves, especially when the decision is an important one, because otherwise their decisions could be misinterpreted and their motives misunderstood.

In real life, it is more likely to be the tone of the message that is altered than the content so that, for example, a polite request reaches its recipient as a curt, imperious summons which is totally self-defeating.

Winners are normally good at communicating insofar as they speak clearly and distinctly with a pleasant easy manner because they know that getting their message across is important. When they can, they deliver the message themselves.

Shame the devil

Winners, as we've already made clear, are not candidates for sainthood, but they do tend to tell the truth, if only out of self-interest, because the truth is easier to remember and it is embarrassingly non-winner to be caught out in a lie. Naturally, winners are no strangers to the face-saving white lie, especially if the face they are saving belongs to someone else. But they also know that truth is bankable and that a reputation for complete truthfulness can come in very handy on those rare occasions when they are forced to be less than candid.

Re-introducing the Jobsworths

If Mr and Mrs Winner and all the little Winners are among the top players in the game of life, then the Jobsworth family are definitely pretty close to the bottom. However, they do have one important function for the intending winner in that they are the perfect example of how not to do things.

We've all met them of course. A great many of the male members of the Jobsworth family, for instance, seem to find occupations which allow them to peer out onto the rest of the world and utter the mournful, distinctive cry of the species: 'Smore than me job's worth.' Other male Jobsworths graduate to positions of authority like foremen, ticket inspectors, minor civil servants and the like but only the accent changes as they intone 'I'm afraid it's more than my job's worth.'

Female Jobsworths can hold all the above jobs but, in addition, are to be found in shops, stores and other places where they can inflict themselves on the general public. Meanwhile, the smaller Jobsworths are busily picking up the family habits, changing from objectionable children who know no other words than, 'Can't', 'Shan't' and 'Won't' into even more despicable teenagers who are already looking for jobs in which their talent for saying 'No' can be exploited to the full. They are also presumably working on the thumbs down techniques they will need in future when they exclaim 'Can't be done, mate' or 'Absolutely out of the question, I'm afraid,' followed by the ritual "Smore than me job's worth.'

Jobsworths never win

Of course the one, and occasionally the only, consoling thing about the Jobsworth tribe is that the jobs, to the worth of which they refer so frequently, are rarely worth very much at all. Jobsworths may think they are winning when they intone their magic phrase and insist on going by the book or their own whim to deliver their totally non-negotiable 'No!' But even though a few unenlightened managers may promote them to positions of cannon fodder executives, whose functions are to take all the flak from below, they will very rarely achieve really important positions and will certainly never become winners.

How to be a winner in a Jobsworth's job

Jobsworths can't win, but a winner in what might be thought of as a typically Jobsworth job can work wonders. Sometimes, they can turn the whole department or the whole factory into winners and win promotions for themselves – if they want it. These are the sort of commissionaires who say 'Hang on, I'll find him for you,' the storekeepers who say 'Let me have a look' and the receptionists who say 'I'll see what I can do.'

Of course, winners are just as likely to come up against the various members of the Jobsworth clan as anyone else but they do seem to have less trouble with them than most other people. This is partly because Jobsworths can usually spot a winner and have well-honed survival instincts which make them anxious to please but mainly because *winners habitually use winning assumptions.*

Winning assumptions

Making winning assumptions is a technique which comes so naturally to winners as to be almost second nature, so much so that many of them use it all the time without being aware that they are doing so. Its function goes far beyond dealing with the infuriating Jobsworth clan but its use in that context makes an interesting example.

A winning assumption consists, quite simply, of taking it for granted that the person you are talking to will be happy to do as you ask. For example, a winner confronted by a Jobsworth receptionist would not say, 'I wonder if I could possibly have a word with Mr Quickstempel,' but something like, 'Good

Morning. My name is Winner, Total Winner and I'm here to see Mr Algernon Quickstempel. Would you be kind enough to tell him I'm here.'

In fact, the assumption lies as much in the tone of voice as in what is said, the tone in this case being friendly but firm and totally confident, without appearing in the least hectoring. In this case, without being much more than reasonably well mannered, the winner has:

- made Jobsworth feel a little bit more human than usual by wishing him a cheery good morning
- established himself as a person whose name is of importance
- stated his business in a positive manner
- conveyed a hint that he may possibly be on first name terms with Mr Quickstempel.

At the same time, he has suggested a course of action to Jobsworth – many of whose family are ditherers – in a way which makes it difficult to refuse.

Beware the pseudo-winner

Winning assumptions are so effective that winners who use them effortlessly have to be careful to avoid exploiting not only the people who work with them, but their own friends and families as well. The danger is that the power, and it is a power, to persuade people to do as one wishes is habit forming – for both parties – and it's very easy to misuse it without even being aware that one is doing so. In extreme cases this can result in a master-slave relationship which no real winner would allow to develop.

However, there are people around who are only too happy to abuse the habit forming aspect of the winning assumption. They are usually people who have read the sort of books on People Management which come with their own chair and whip. Their method is to use winning assumptions to gain not a rapport, but dominance. They are often to be found in the workplace where they tend to practise this form of manipulation on people of equal or slightly lower rank to themselves.

Winners will use one of their big guns – humour – against such operators, without even having to refuse their minor requests. For example, the attempt to make the intended victim into an 'obvious' messenger recoils when the recipient is told with a grin, 'that idle blighter Smartarse asked me to drop these off.'

The difference between the pseudo-winner who deliberately sets out to dominate, and the real winner who has everyone from the office cleaner to the Managing Director doing him favours, is one of the nuances of the winning game and can be seen clearly only in the light of the way other people react.

Winners never leave people feeling that they have been conned – except in the nicest possible way.

Winners can say 'no'!

Winners like to say 'yes' but this doesn't mean they are pushovers and they can say 'no' if they have to. However, they do so pleasantly. We know of one major company who employed a professional letter writer especially to write 'difficult' letters. He was reputed to be so good that he could write a letter of dismissal which made the recipient feel great about getting the sack.

Using the tape recorder, try your hand at saying 'no' to several different requests while making the other person feel a winner. Then write a couple of letters of dismissal, one beginning, say, 'This is to notify you . . .' and the other on the lines of 'Dear Bill, I have felt for some time now that you have not been completely happy here at Bloggs Brothers and, although we shall be sorry to see you go...'

Winners are friendly

Being cheerful and friendly makes all the difference in your relationships with others because being friendly shows that you care. You care about the person you are talking to, you care about his or her problems and you care about helping to solve these problems.

Some organisations train their employees in improving the quality of customer or client care and this type of people training is becoming increasingly important. It is also becoming increasingly specialised.

But if you want to sum up the technical jargon relating to this change of attitude in one word, then that word is 'friendliness'.

It shows that you care for people and therefore care for your customers. Sales people talk to the actual customer. But the secret is to get all employees thinking of their colleague as a customer, the next department as a customer and so on. The benefit is a more friendly organisation, a more winning organisation and of course it is the real customers who pay our salaries.

There is a short term risk that if you are too friendly, non-winners will take advantage of you so you have to learn to spot this situation when it occurs. Non-winning bosses of the autocratic type sometimes mistake friendliness for weakness. But even autocrats can be winners and it may be useful to ask yourself 'Is he a just bastard – or is he just a bastard?'

Winners will always win in the long run. Being a winner means that, not only do *you* not behave like a bastard, you don't even have to feel like a bastard … and that's only one of the advantages of being a winner, as we shall see when we look into the payoff, the million pound question of *what's in it for me?*

Tip from the Top

CUSTOMERS ...

... are the most important people in our business

... are not dependent on us – we depend on them

... are not people to argue or match wits with

... deserve the best treatment we can give them because it's money that pays salaries.

13

What's In It for Me?

Okay – so you've decided to become a winner, or perhaps more of a winner than you already are. You've made up your mind to try at least some of the things we've suggested so far, both in the workplace and away from it, mainly because everyone likes to see themselves as poised and confident and it's intriguing to think that you can train yourself to be a winner.

However, at the same time, you are almost certainly asking yourself, 'What's the bottom line? It's all very well asking us to do all these things, to behave in this way, to speak to people in such a way but, after all – what's in it for me?'

The glittering prizes

Well, as a winner, you will almost certainly be fitter, more attractive, happier and will live longer – which isn't bad for starters. You could also be more successful and make a lot of money. As we've pointed out, in the game of life there are more prizes than people, and winning can become a habit.

Fitter? Well, we've already talked about becoming fitter but being a winner brings its own fitness bonuses because, as a winner, you are less likely to be stressed, less likely to suffer from heart disease, to become an alcoholic or smoke too much. Winning also gives you tremendous energy – watch the winning team run a lap of honour while the losers collapse exhausted – so you feel fitter all the time. Again, there are those captains of industry, some of them quite elderly, who have a reputation for tireless energy and tackle a punishing work schedule that leaves their younger executives running to keep up. Their secret is that they aren't really working – they are winners who are thoroughly enjoying themselves. As a winner, say the safety experts, you are also less likely than other people to have an accident either in the workplace or elsewhere, which could also add to your life span.

All it takes is a smile

As we've mentioned, winners do tend to smile a great deal and according to the British Safety Council smiling and laughter can reduce accidents, help performance at work and add years to your life. Smiling will help you to lead a happier, stress-free life. Smile and you're on your way to becoming a winner.

Happier? Well, winning is enjoyable so you will certainly be happier as a winner. As a winner you'll look forward to going to work as an opportunity to demonstrate your skills or expertise, perhaps to earn praise and to increase your self-esteem. You'll also enjoy meeting your colleagues and fellow winners, fellow members of a winning team.

Feeling good about going to work is a major win because we spend approximately a third of our lives at work, plus more hours getting to and from work and, frequently, more hours thinking about work in our 'spare' time. Losers try to switch off when they set off for work and remain switched off, or at least put their brains on automatic until they get home again. They certainly don't enjoy the intervening period; often they actually hate it, which means they are wasting their lives. This is why *winning at work gives us back half of our waking lives.*

Winners are more attractive?

It sounds a bit like an ad. 'Be more attractive to your colleagues, to the boss, to the opposite sex!' but, in fact, winners *are* more attractive people than losers. Would you rather spend time with a happy winner or a miserable grouch of a loser? Certainly, winners tend to be more attractive to the opposite sex than losers and, even if some losers collect the sympathy vote, it is rarely the basis of a good relationship.

Winners have a better sex-life?

Certainly. Sex, in fact, is a perfect example of non-competitive winning in which you become a winner by making sure that the other person wins, thus creating a winning partnership. Married winners extend this winning partnership to cover all aspects of their lives and are frequently described by other people as 'lucky' but, while they are certainly fortunate, luck as such doesn't necessarily have much to do with it. It is simply that the winner's confidence and self-esteem means they don't feel the need to dominate their partners and a genuine shared relationship becomes possible, giving winners a good chance of a happy marriage and, best of all, of a happy, well-adjusted family with kids who pick up winning habits from the outset. In other words, a marriage – like a person – can be 'happy in its skin'.

Winners are richer and more successful?

At last, the nitty gritty, the bottom line, the nub, the pith, the essence. After all, it's all very well talking about motivation but what about the money?

Well, winners do tend to be at the very least comfortable in the financial sense – although, for short periods at least, and especially if they know the situation to be only temporary, they can manage with less than other people. Being broke can be a challenge to a winner, provided he or she knows that help is available if needed.

Being permanently unemployed, and hopelessly so – which is, we suppose, the nearest one can get to real poverty in this country without opting out of the system – is very different, but here again winners have built-in resources which nobody can take away from them.

On one housing estate in Glasgow virtually everyone was unemployed until recently. Most of them, understandably, had sunk into complete apathy and depression but one man had spent his time doing up his house and garden and tending an allotment which supplied the family with all the fruit and vegetables they needed. He had also taken up watch repairing as a potentially remunerative hobby and was teaching himself French. In addition to all this, he was also spending a specific amount of time per week in an active search for a job and there seemed little doubt that of all the men on the estate, he would be first to be employed. In the meantime, unemployed or not, he was a happy man – and a winner.

In the main, however, winners do succeed in the workplace – after all, who would you rather employ, a winner who could make the department, the office or the workshop a winner, or a loser who would infect his colleagues with his own loser's gloom? More to the point, who would you rather promote?

It is the winner's power to inspire others to win as much as anything else which makes him or her a natural leader and in the workplace this brings rewards in terms of money and prestige.

Winners make good bosses

Real winners make splendid bosses and this is something that any Managing Director who is himself a winner will appreciate – which, of course, is one way in which winning permeates the whole organisation. One reason they are such good bosses is that they allow every member of the team to make a contribution and acknowledge its importance. This doesn't mean that decisions are taken by committee.

One reason winners earn promotion and success in the workplace is that they are perceived to be winners. They have created a winning persona which is accepted by their colleagues, and their bosses and, where applicable, by the general public.

Sporting winners for instance become TV personalities, successful actors become politicians – even presidents – and politicians become successful authors, all because winners in one field are perceived as potential winners in other spheres. This is sometimes a little unfair on people who may be as well or better qualified than the chosen winners when it comes to the winners' secondary occupation – for example when sports stars get plum TV jobs. But it is a fact of life that winners get more chances to show what they are capable of than other people.

Winners get more chances

We've already pointed out that even winning at tiddlywinks will help you get the winning habit and that this will help you to become a winner elsewhere. But obviously if you are thinking of an outside win that will help make you a career winner, you should try to make it more job related.

An external degree or an Open University degree, for example, will be a useful demonstration of your winning abilities whatever discipline you choose. So if that's what you decide to do, pick a course that really interests you.

Mastering job-related skills is another form of outside winning which could bring career success but, again, pick something that you want to do for the fun of it. If you do a lot of driving in your job you could think about taking an advanced driving course as a source of satisfaction and, incidentally, as a talking point for your colleagues and bosses. Real winners aren't pushy but they are not anonymous either, especially in the workplace.

If you work in a job where not all the people in a similar job to yourself are personally known to the individual who does the promoting, it is obvious that to be a career success – if that's what you have in mind – you need to be among those who are known, if only as the person who is learning Sanskrit or Origami. Even if you make no special effort on the career front and are happy just to be a winner in the workplace and elsewhere, simply content to get as much enjoyment as possible out of doing the job well, you are going to stand out from the crowd and one way and another you will find it difficult to avoid promotion, success, money and the rest.

Winners have these things thrust upon them.

So – that's it then?

Well, you might be forgiven for thinking that when it comes to the 'What's in it for me?' bit, the foregoing is, as it were, it. After all, if becoming a winner can make you happier, fitter, more attractive, richer and more successful, not to mention helping you to live longer, it has to be well worth doing. In fact, however, there's a great deal more to it than that because winning is not only life-extending but immensely life-enhancing.

Taking charge of our lives, even if we only make a start by getting up a few minutes earlier than other people dictate, places us firmly among the 'doers' of this world.

Winning is life-enhancing

Remember the old joke about the man who went to the doctor and was given the sad news that he had not long to live? The doctor advised him to give up drinking, smoking, sex, music and television. 'Will that help me live longer?' he asked eagerly, to which the doctor replied 'I'm afraid not – but it will seem longer.'

The point is that, while any sort of life is usually worth clinging on to, it is the quality of life that is really important, whether we measure the quality of our lives in terms of fine wine, country walks or great art – and winning improves the quality of life immensely. One of the best examples of a winner we know is a woman who manages a family, has a successful career as a writer and in addition runs a luxury hotel renowned for its food. As a genuine winner, she is totally happy with her life, a great deal of the success of which is due to the fact that people like her. As a bonus she is able to choose as her guests the sort of people she describes as 'life enhancers', so that her house parties and dinners are gatherings of interesting and amusing winners.

The fact that, in addition, she is being paid to do what she likes doing and does well puts her in a typical winner's situation.

Winning is magic

'Give me Generals who are lucky' said Napoleon, meaning of course generals who were winners, generals who achieved victories with what seemed magic. Nowadays, people say of winners that he or she has 'the magic touch' because they are the ones for whom everything seems to go not only right but splendidly and, in fact, there is a touch of magic about being a winner. You can feel it every time you make a winning move – a pleasant tingle if the win is an everyday bit of winmanship or a great rush of euphoria if it's a biggie, better than booze and pretty nearly as good as sex. Like booze, it can induce everything from sheer contentment to a feeling of invincibility but, unlike booze, there's no hangover and both the feeling of content and the knowledge that you are likely to succeed in anything you undertake are real – and that's magic. Best of all, of course, it's the sort of magic that can be acquired by almost anyone and we hope we've provided a few useful guidelines if not a magic wand. So start winning *now*. It could well be the beginning of a winning streak that will last for the rest of your life.

Index